I0492520

Can companies do well by doing good?

The role of leadership in embedding CSR into corporate culture

Murat Guvenc

Copyright © 2017 by Murat Guvenc

All rights reserved. No part of this publication may be reproduced, distributed or transmitted in any form or by any means, including photocopying, recording, or other electronic or mechanical methods, without the prior written permission of the author, except in the case of brief quotations embodied in critical reviews and certain other noncommercial uses permitted by copyright law.

Published 2017

ISBN-10: 1981464220

ISBN-13: 978-1981464227

Cover Design by Adara Su Guvenc

Contents

Part I – Introduction

Introduction

To date, a majority of organizations have adopted CSR as a strategy and rolled out several CSR projects world-wide. Yet, many of those CSR projects are challenged to bring the value they promised due to lack of alignment, focus and other reasons. It is often debated whether companies have a pursuable strategy to build CSR in the genies of corporate culture, or it is mostly used as a PR tool, driven by corporate headquarter, not embedded in daily operations and lacking full employee engagement.

Although many studies can be found on the topic of leadership and the role of leadership in development and execution of company-wide strategic initiatives such as CSR, very little work has been done to measure the influence of leadership on executing CSR strategy successfully in multi-national organizations and relatively few studies examined an organization's readiness at employee level.

The purpose of this study is to address this gap and develop a framework – 'CAAVE' - to analyze the effectiveness of leadership in five dimensions;

- Culture - Is CSR integrated into corporate culture?
- Awareness - Are employees aware of and knowledgeable in CSR concepts?
- Attitude - Are employees motivated to participate and support CSR activities?
- Visibility - Is CSR visible within the organization?
- Engagement - Do employees have responsibility and accountability for CSR

By parametrizing the behavior in five dimensions, the study aims to formulate a model that can be used to measure and benchmark an organization's internal CSR readiness at employee and organizational level, and identify the possible gaps to maximize the impact of CSR programs.

The book is organized in five sections. In the first section, I introduce the key drivers that made CSR an essential part of corporate strategy (Chapter 1) and discuss the challenges embedding CSR into business strategy (Chapter 2).

In the second part, I introduce the broader concept of CSR (Chapter 3), provide examples from companies which have reputation with successful CSR implementations (Chapter 4) and discuss the leadership theories and leadership's role in CSR (Chapter 5).

In the third section, I highlight the findings on three controversial topics; whether social performance can be measured (Chapter 6), whether CSR activities can positively affect company's value (Chapter 7), and whether consumers care about CSR (Chapter 8).

In the fourth section, I briefly present my research design methodology (Chapter 9), followed by my findings (Chapter 10).

In the last section, I summarize my conclusions (Chapter 11).

Chapter 1 - Why does CSR become a key corporate issue?

During the past decade, the stakeholders; customers, employees, investors, suppliers, non-government organizations are getting more and more conscious and demanding with their view that obligations of companies should go beyond generating profits. A company has responsibility to both shareholders and all stakeholders which means that it has responsibility to all society [42, pg.85]. As a result of this, CSR has become a key component of corporate strategy.

The urgency of the stakeholders' rising demand for pushing companies to act more responsibly is **mainly driven by global risks** as defined by climate change (increase in global temperature, sea level rise, ocean acidification), environmental degradation (fresh water scarcity, loss of biodiversity), poverty and rising inequalities among countries, and to certain extend the loss of public trust in public companies (scandals of Enron, Worldcom, Lehman Brothers, and Volkswagen lately). The recent developments such as the declaration of United Nations 2030 agenda for sustainable development in Sep 2015 [98] and the adoption of the Paris Agreement on 12 December 2015 by 195 governments, reemphasize the criticality of the situation and sets a major turning point of collective recognition of the dangerous risks posed by climate change as well as the cost of inaction [95, pg.19].

World Economic Forum conducted a survey reaching out 750 experts and decision makers from business, academia, civil society and the public sector,

11

asking respondents to rate global risks over a ten-year time horizon. The failure of climate change mitigation and adaptation and water crises were perceived as the most impactful risk for the years to come, reconfirming the urgency that has raised by UN. The findings are summarized in "Global Risks Report 2016".

Figure 1.1 – The Global Risks Landscape 2016 [96, pg.3]

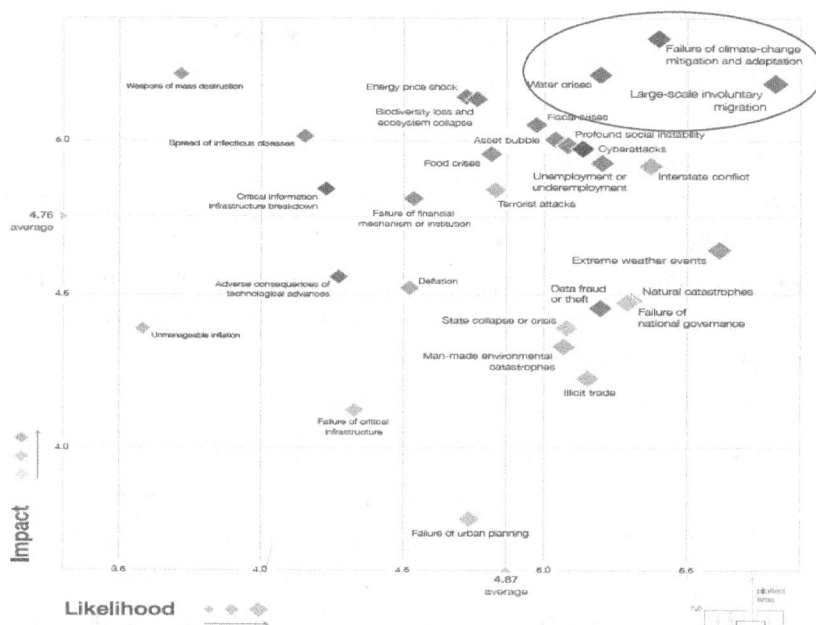

In order to respond to the global risks, companies, both large and small, have modified their strategies to consider governmental regulations, stakeholder interests, and evolving societal and environmental expectations [46, pg.9]. So, it is no longer acceptable for a company to say that the conditions under which their suppliers operate is outside their control and, so they are not responsible [42, pg.20]. During 2008 conference of World Economic Forum, Kellie McElhaney pointed out the importance CSR in today's business environment; "*If your company doesn't already have a CSR strategy or CSR initiatives, it likely soon will, as it has become standard operating procedure*

for today's companies." [7, pg.1]

We can confirm the positive trend by looking at the number of companies listed in S&P 500 market index which adopted sustainability reporting recently. As illustrated in the following diagram, the ratio rose from 20% in 2011 to 81% in 2015. [63]

Figure 1.2 – S&P 500 Companies Sustainability Reporting

Governance & Accountability Institute Research Results
S&P 500® Companies Sustainability Reporting
▪ Reporters   ▪ Non-Reporters

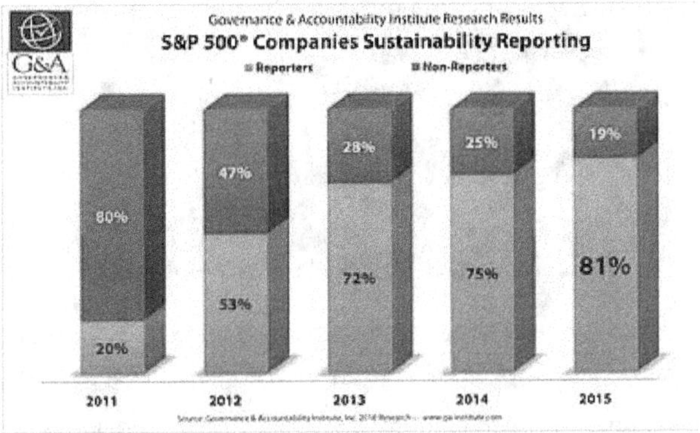

[63]

In addition to this positive trend, we also observe that there is clearly a shift in corporate attitudes from '**doing good to look good**' to '**doing well and doing good**'. Initiatives are moved from short-term charitable donations to long-term value creation, and more integrated to strategic business goals and objectives [9, pg. 4-9]. In her keynote at the Business for Social Responsibility Annual Conference, former HP Chairman and CEO Carly Fiorina confirmed this view saying that "*For many years, community development goals were philanthropic activities that were seen as separate from business objectives, not fundamental to them; doing well and doing good were seen as separate pursuits. But I think that is changing.*" [20] As a result, CSR is no longer just about charity or philanthropy. It is doing better than basics. It is doing better than legally required.

Furthermore, another reason why CSR became a key activity is the belief that sustainability is good for business and could help corporations differentiate their services or products and possibly lead to generation of new revenue stream. According to CEO study done in 2013, about 80% of global CEOs see sustainability as the root to growth in innovation and leading to competitive advantage in their industries.

Figure 1.3 – CEO Study on Sustainability [75, min:4:07]

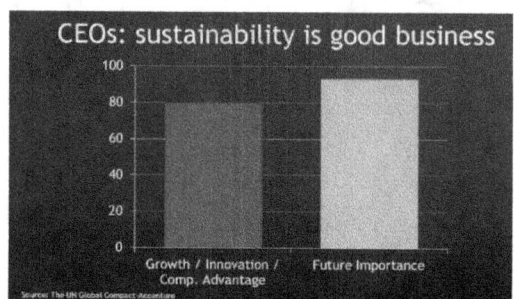

Another study done by UN Global Compact-Accenture in 2016, supports the same view. According to survey results, 97% of CEOs believe that sustainability is important to the future success of their business [50, pg.3]. Many companies are making a conscious effort to put sustainable practices into action not only to help the environment and society, but also to create goodwill for their reputations and contribute positively to their brands' health and performance [27, pg.3]. So, the views of CEOs are clear. There is tremendous opportunity in sustainability.

A study done by IBM Institute for Business Value surveying a group of 250 business leaders worldwide, revealed that two-thirds (68%) are focusing on CSR activities <u>to create new revenue streams</u>. According to IBM's report, <u>when aligned with business objectives, companies are beginning to see that CSR can bring competitive differentiation</u>, permission to enter new markets, and favorable positioning in the talent wars. More than half (54%) of the business leaders believe that their companies' CSR activities are already giving them an advantage over their top competitors. [8]

Last but not least, the Reputation Institute estimates that <u>CSR impacts 40% of</u>

the brand image value [6]. According to Reputation Institute, reputation is an emotional bond that brings many benefits;

Figure 1.4 – Benefits of CSR by Reputation Institute

Reputation is an emotional bond...

... that ensures

* **Consumers** use your products

* **Customers** recommend you

* Your **investors** support you

* **Policy-makers** and **regulators** give you the benefit of the doubt

* Your **employees** are aligned and deliver on your strategy

[24, pg.7]

As a summary, CSR is becoming more mainstream as many companies begin to embed CSR initiatives into the core of their business operations. With globalization, corporations have to extend their CSR policies not only to their overseas subsidiaries but also to suppliers. Some companies only do what they are legally required to do, but many go beyond the minimum required as they feel accountable to shareholders, to employees, to suppliers and to society as a whole. There is a shift from obligation to strategy. Companies with the right CSR strategy in place, can increase profitability, boost innovation, improve brand reputation, and differentiate their offering from competitors by developing positive relationships with all the key stakeholders.

Can companies do well by doing good?

Chapter 2 - What are the challenges with CSR?

Despite the popularity of CSR and growing number of emphasis put on CSR initiatives, companies struggle with the fundamental challenge of embedding CSR into day-to-day business strategy [7]. Some companies look at CSR more as a fashionable trend rather than a coherent practical program, resulting in low commitment and investment and having most CSR initiatives being understaffed [19, 403]. CSR in most businesses is typically executed in a very <u>ad hoc, non-integrated fashion</u> and often not directly linked to what the firm actually knows, does, or is expert in [7]. CSR team is an isolated department for which no one else in the organization feels responsible.

According to Reputation Institute, companies with strong CSR reputation have four characteristics in common; their CSR strategy is <u>well aligned with their business model</u>, they have <u>strong leadership</u> support, they <u>focus on projects with real impact</u> on society rather than corporate philanthropy and they have <u>full engagement</u> of employees and other stakeholders [24, pg.22]. A global survey done Nielsen revealed comparable results suggesting that to succeed in CSR, companies need to have a

17

clear and actionable vision, endorsement by leadership team, consistent messaging, accountability and measurement [27, pg.13]. A study commissioned by Industry Canada, shows that high performing CSR organizations foster a culture of CSR and fully integrate CSR throughout their operations, rewarding and incentivizing CSR decisions and initiatives [103, pg.2] and the critical success factors for implementing CSR include having an overarching vision that includes CSR, having senior management and board level commitment, engaged staff and the provision of skills, tools and incentives [103, pg.6].

TCC Group, a consulting firm focused on corporate citizenship, developed a framework for successful CSR. The framework highlights four key elements as illustrated in below.

Figure 2.1 – Framework for Successful Corporate Citizenship

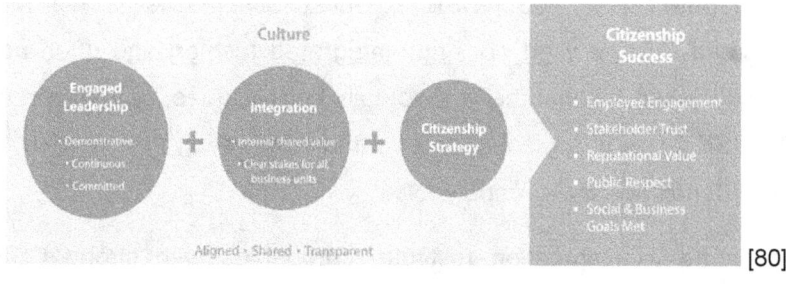

[80]

In the nutshell, TCC states that successful companies have clear goals. They have strong measurement and reporting systems that ensure senior leaders are tracking progress against goals. They run high impact programs that are supported by an integrated structure, but most importantly, their leaders are genuinely committed, and their culture aligns with their values.

In his book, "Green Giants", F. Williams (2015) gave examples of companies who demonstrated great economic success while implementing sustainable principles. Williams pinpointed <u>six traits</u> that those companies have in common that set them apart from other companies [91];

- iconoclastic leadership
- disruptive innovation
- a higher purpose
- sustainability being integrated into core business strategy
- mainstream appeal
- a new behavioral contract

<u>As a summary</u>, while all the elements discussed above are equally important for the success of CSR, many of them are linking back to the effective role of leadership, as leaders are primarily responsible for setting the organization's policy on CSR and preparing the organization for implementing the CSR vision and strategy.

Can companies do well by doing good?

Part II – CSR Overview

Can companies do well by doing good?

Chapter 3 - What is CSR?

CSR is not a new concept. The origin of CSR is tracing back to 1950s and it became popularized in 1970s. The concept of CSR has evolved in years from philanthropy focusing community-based programs and employment rights, into a broader concept of integrating social and environmental responsibilities into business operations, and it still continues to develop. One of the challenges with CSR as stated by Votaw (1973) is that **the term means something, but not always the same thing to everybody**. Over the years CSR term is used interchangeably with other terms including sustainability, corporate citizenship, social entrepreneurship, corporate accountability, corporate philanthropy, business ethics, etc. Although many of these terms are overlapping with each other and time to time used synonymously, there are still differences between them.

S. O. Idowu, W. L. Filho (2009) summarized the relationship, where 'corporate citizenship' is a component of CSR, the later addressing wider issues of society and environment. 'Sustainability' integrates the economic dimension at the macro-level perspective.

Figure 3.1 – Sustainability Relationship Matrix

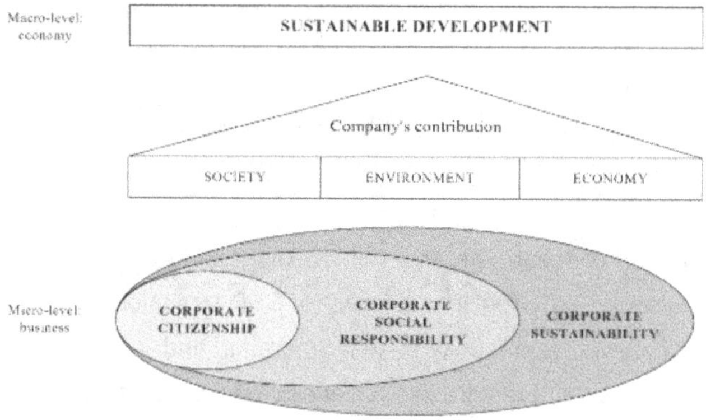

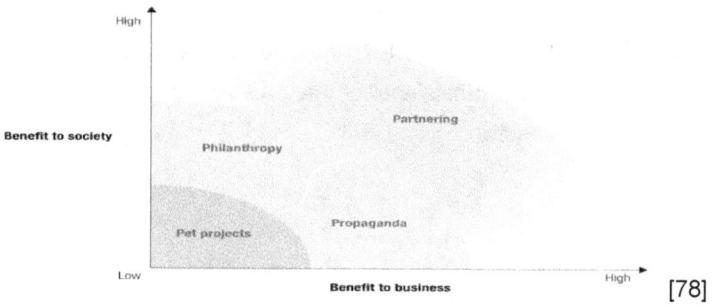

[114, pg.66]

CSR emphasizes the responsibility of corporations to make money and as well the responsibility to interact ethically with the surrounding community [15, pg.665]. In that respect, **CSR encompasses dual objectives**; pursuing benefits for the business and for society as illustrated below.

Figure 3.2 – CSR Landscape

[78]

A good definition of CSR is done by P. Kotler and N. Lee; "*CSR is a commitment to improve community well-being through discretionary business practices and contributions of corporate resources*", where the key element in

24

this definition is the word <u>discretionary</u> which is referring to business activities that are not mandated by law or that are moral or ethical in nature, but <u>rather a voluntary commitment</u> a business makes in choosing and implementing these practices and making these contributions [9, pg.3]. The voluntary aspect is rephrased by Commission of the European Communities, where CSR is defined as a concept whereby companies integrate social and environmental concerns in their business operations and in their interaction with their stakeholders <u>on a voluntary basis</u> [3, pg.19].

CSR, in more simplified terms, is a form of <u>corporate self-regulation</u> where a business monitors and ensures its active compliance with the spirit of the law, ethical standards and national or international norms.

In general, <u>corporations have four responsibilities</u>;

- economic responsibility to make money
- legal responsibility to adhere to rules and regulations
- ethical responsibility to do what's right even when not required by the law
- philanthropic responsibility to contribute to society's projects

CSR provides a set of business practices to work with stakeholders in achieving those responsibilities by improving economic, environmental and social performance, known as the **triple bottom line**. Carroll (1991) organized CSR as a four-layered pyramid model and called it the pyramid of responsibilities. <u>Carroll's CSR Pyramid</u> is probably the most well-known model of CSR, with its four levels indicating the relative importance of economic, legal, ethical and philanthropic responsibilities respectively. According to Carroll, CSR involves the conduct of a business so that it is economically profitable, law abiding, ethical and socially supportive [18, pg.4].

Figure 3.3 – Carroll's CSR Pyramid

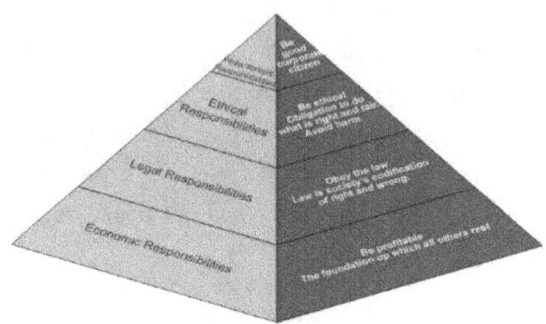

Carroll's CSR Pyramid

The same view is presented by M. Kramer a little bit differently. According to Kramer, there are four prevailing justification for CSR, which somehow intersects with Carrol's pyramid of responsibilities; legal – license to operate, ethical – sustainability, philanthropic – moral obligation and economic – enhancing reputation.

Figure 3.4 – Four Prevailing Justifications for CSR

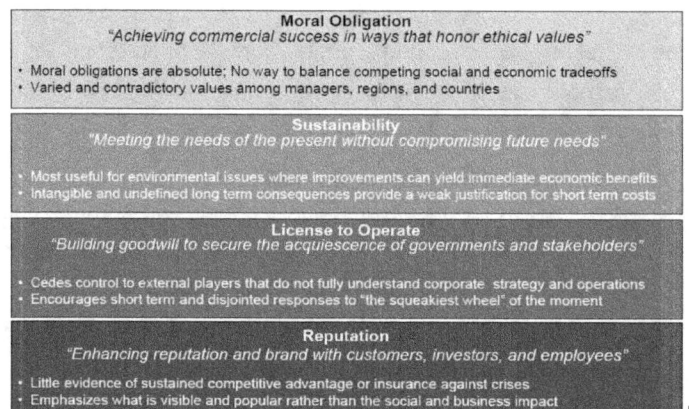

[31, pg. 2]

As stated by Werther and Chandler (2006), the rationale for CSR can be based on a moral argument, a rational argument, or an economic argument

[35, pg.4]. CSR activities are typically divided among three practices;

- **Philanthropic** – They do not to produce profits or directly improve business performance [32, pg.3]. Practices range from donating money, services, or products to non-profit organizations, charities, partnering with organizations to raise public awareness on certain issues, granting scholarships to students, offering technical expertise, knowledge, and skills, and more [23, pg.10].

- **Business practices** – They deliver social or environmental benefits in a way that support a company's operations across the value chain, often improving efficiency and effectiveness [32, pg.3]. They may generate revenue or reduce costs. Practices include participating in environmental projects, reducing waste, implementing a recycling program, implementing global take-back program, switching to use renewable energy sources, etc. [23, pg.11].

- **Innovation** – They create new forms of business specifically to address social or environmental challenges [32, pg.3-4]. CSR activities inherent in products.

From a different perspective, Michael E. Porter developed a CSR framework in collaboration with Foundation Strategy Group, dividing CSR activities into four categories [46, pg.11];

- **Compliance** - Create societal benefits in conformance with local legal standards.

- **Best practices** - Create additional societal benefits motivated by the values of the owner or the expectations of society.

- **Innovation** - Develop new products or services that offer societal benefits as a specific part of the customer value proposition.

- **Voluntary support** - Contributions of money, time, products, or services.

In a broader scope, D. Hessekiel, the founder of Companies & Causes Canada [14] and P. Kotler and N. Lee, the author of the book of "Good Works", defined six categories for corporate social initiatives;

- **Cause promotion** - Leverages corporate funds to increase awareness and concern about a social cause or to support fundraising, participation, or volunteer recruitment for a cause.

- **Cause Related Marketing** - Links monetary or in-kind donations to product sales or other consumer action.

- **Corporate Social Marketing** - Uses business resources to develop and/or implement a behavioural change intended to improve public health, safety, the environment, or community well-being.

- **Corporate Philanthropy** - Involves a corporation making a direct contribution to a charity, most often in the form of cash grants, donations, and in-kind services.

- **Employee Engagement** - Encourage employees to engage with non-profit organizations by volunteering their expertise, talents, ideas and physical labour.

- **Socially Responsible Business Practices** - Discretionary business practices, not mandated by law or regulations that a corporation adopts to support social causes in order to improve community well-being and protect the environment.

According to Murray & Vogel (1997) companies face demands from a wide range of internal and external stakeholders, which can affect an organization negatively or positively. [62, pg.9] M. Bhandarkar and T. A. Rivero defined four actors that put pressure on companies for change as illustrated in the diagram below.

Figure 3.5 – CSR Actors

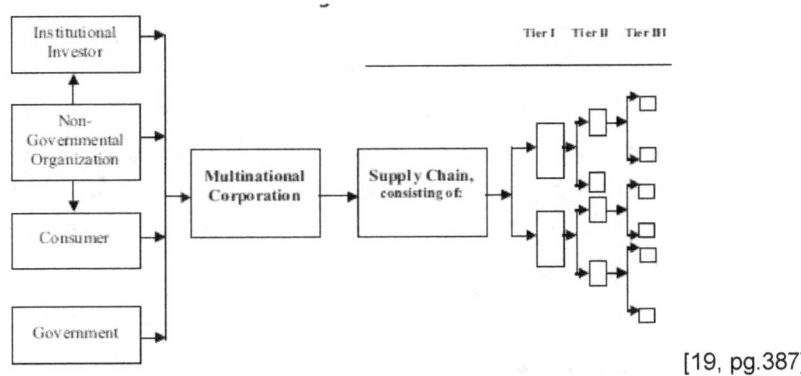

[19, pg.387]

Among those four actors, <u>customers/consumers are rated as the biggest external driver</u>, based on a study done by Centre for Corporate Citizenship at Boston College for US companies.

Figure 3.6 – US National Survey - Drivers for Corporate Citizenship

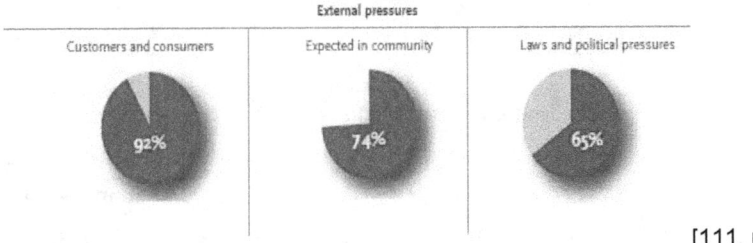

[111, pg.18]

Business leaders believe that **consumers** are critical actors to drive change in sustainable living (environmental, social and governance) issues. According to the 2015 Edelman Trust Barometer, 84% of consumers believe that business can pursue its own goals while simultaneously doing good for society [10, pg.11]. Reputation Institute revelated the fact that consumers are 15 times more willing to recommend a company with an excellent CSR reputation [24, pg.12]. Also, the downside of behaving unethically is much greater as a negative image of CSR can damage consumer's valuation more than what a positive image can improve.

29

Government is another influencer to pressure businesses to change their behavior. Governments typically exert pressure in areas related to employment conditions and pollution [19, pg.389] and mandate social responsibility reporting [30, pg.3]. The findings of a study conducted in 2016 jointly by KPMG International, GRI and United Nations Environment Program (UNEP) covering 71 countries supported the influence of governments and regulators by encouraging companies to disclose sustainability information in their annual reports, and as a result there has been a surge in the number of reporting instruments identified; 383 versus 180 instruments as illustrated below.

Figure 3.7 – Trends in Sustainability Reporting Instruments

		2006		2010		2013		2016	
Reporting Instruments	Mandatory	35	58%	94	62%	130	72%	248	65%
	Voluntary	25	42%	57	38%	50	28%	135	35%
	Total	60		151		180		383	
Countries & Regions		19		32		44		71 (64 with instruments)	

[44, pg.6]

Another example of this endorsement is, effective as of December 6th, 2014, there is a new directive for European Union member states which requires companies with 500 or more employees to disclose in their management reports information on policies, social and employee aspects, risks and outcomes regarding environmental matter. [62, pg.1]

Yet, P. Polman, the chief executive of Unilever, is skeptical on this view and pointed out that it is very difficult to get long-term commitment from governments due to fact that countries are in political stasis as a result of elections or leadership changes. "*Governments are coming out of office almost on a weekly basis, so the onus is on companies to lead the way.*" [29]

The third stakeholder **NGOs**, activist organizations and media also play as a key role. Companies do not exist in vacuum. As P. Polman, CEO of Unilever said "*It will take much more than one company, government or community to solve the challenges that face us. We need entirely new types of collaboration, innovation and partnership between these bodies if we are to drive collective action for a brighter and more sustainable future for all.*" [43, pg.3] Companies should develop **innovative partnership** with non-profit organizations, where non-profits can provide valuable insights on emerging issues and help companies focus on the right initiatives. With better collaboration with non-profits, companies can create more value than they could do apart.

One good example of the influence of non-profits is the case in which Greenpeace's exerted pressure on Nestlé's use of palm oil in its products. Palm oil is crucial ingredient in many consumer products, but the increased world demand of the product has been linked with extensive deforestation of rainforests for palm oil production. In 2009, Greenpeace encouraged a boycott for Nestlé KitKat chocolate bars to put pressure on the company to adopt a more sustainable supply chain in terms of the company's sourcing of palm oil used in the product. [62, pg.10] Another example is Apple, where the company faced claims that their contractors are forcing staff to do overtime involuntarily and employing underage workers at the factory [64]. As a result of facing pressure by public responses, many organizations go beyond the basic regulatory requirements of its operations and began to act into societal problems.

It is also important to note that there is a significant increase in the number of non-profits in the recent decades as seen in the graph below.

Figure 3.8 – Growth of International Nongovernmental Organizations

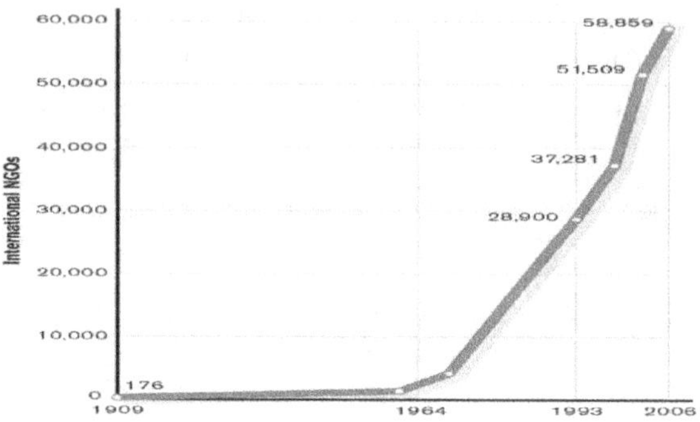

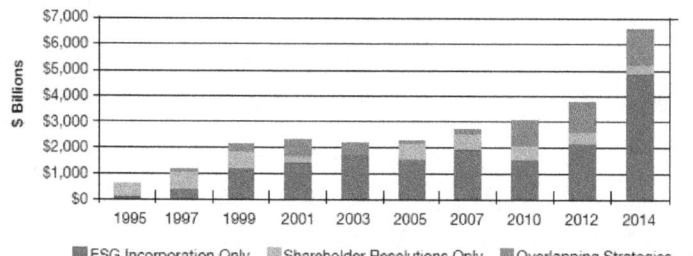

[90]

There are number of NGOs that are very vocal and influencer in support to development and endorsement of CSR. Some of those reference organizations are listed in "Appendix B".

Socially responsible investing (SRI), the practice of investors who think ethically and socially about which stocks to buy, sell, or avoid, has grown substantially over the past years. The Social Investment Forum estimates that SRI presently makes up 5-10% of all stock market investments in US [11, pg.56]. That means, one in every ten dollars was invested in companies that rate high on some measure of social responsibility.

Figure 3.9 – Sustainable and Responsible Investing in US 1995–2014

[37, pg.12]

Harvard Business School conducted a research and they found that if one had invested a dollar 20 years ago in a portfolio of companies that focused narrowly on making more money quarter by quarter, that one dollar would

32

have grown to 14 dollars and 46 cents. If instead one had invested that same dollar in a portfolio of companies that focused on growing their business and on the most important environmental and social issues, that one dollar would have grown to 28 dollars and 36 cents, almost twice.

Figure 3.10 – HBS Study on ROI in Socially Responsible Companies

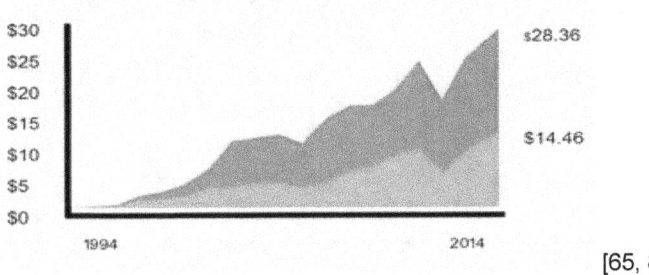

[65, 8:05]

The previous two data prove that there is a growing demand from individual and institutional investors and as well opportunity in investing in companies which are incorporating environmental, social and governance (ESG) factors into their business. Environment includes energy consumption, water availability, waste and pollution, just making <u>efficient uses of resources</u>. Social includes human capital, things like employee engagement and innovation capacity, as well as supply chain management and labor rights and human rights. And governance relates to the oversight of companies by their boards and investors. The PRI, an international network of investor, has grown consistently since it began in 2006.

Figure 3.11 – Asset Growth of PRI

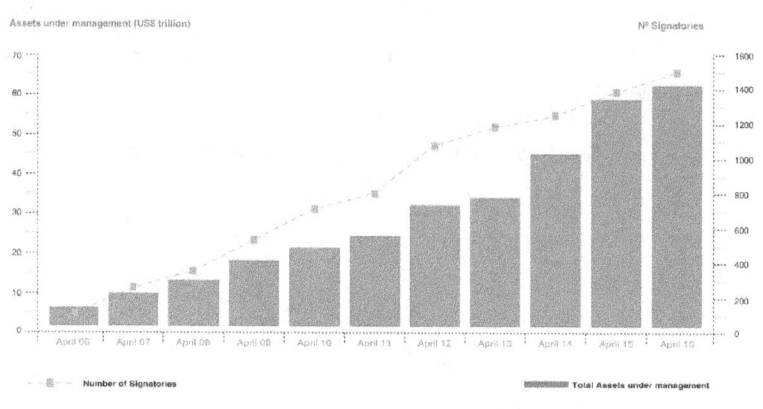

[47]

Another key stakeholder, although missing in the M. Bhandarkar and T. A. Rivero diagram is the **employees**. Employees have three main motives to engage in CSR [109, pg.4];

- instrumental (self-interest driven)
- relational (concerned with relationships among group members)
- moral (concerned with ethical standards and moral principles)

A CSR study conducted by the Society for Human Resource Management in 2006, reveals that CSR practices are seen important to employee morale (50%), loyalty (41%), and retention (29%) [103, pg.6]. According to survey done by Kelly Services in 2009, employees are prepared to sacrifice pay or promotion in order to work for organizations that are actively engaged in good social responsibility practices. Almost 90% of respondents say they are more likely to work for an organization that is considered ethically and socially responsible [48]. Younger generations or millennials, who will make up half the workforce by 2024 according to Gartner, want to work for responsible employers that offer community engagement opportunities. Robert E. Moritz, Chairman and Senior Partner of PwC U.S., noted that "*Millennials don't only demand to know the organization's purpose but are also prepared to leave the firm if that purpose doesn't align with their own values."* [10, pg.11]

According to survey done by Reputation Institute, potential employees are 14 times more willing to work for a company with an excellent CSR reputation vs. a weak [24, pg.12]. More than two-thirds (67%) of respondents in Nielsen's annual global online survey on CSR say that they prefer to work for a socially responsible company [27, pg.3].

Looking at the results of all the studies done above, we can drive to conclusion that CSR is essential in **attracting and retaining top talent** and has a positive impact in employee motivation to yield better performance.

Can companies do well by doing good?

Chapter 4 – Examples of Successful CSR Initiatives

There are many notable examples of sustainable corporate actions that impose positive impact on communities and environment. Some companies focus on environmental issues such as deforestation, decreasing CO_2 emission and zero waste programs, some restructure the entire value chain to ensure sustainable development and fair trade, some donate medical drugs and vaccines in support to Third World nations, and some become an advocate in child labor. In the table below, there is a small set of CSR initiatives categorized in reference to D. Hessekiel, P. Kotler and N. Lee, that have been successfully implemented in the past years and demonstrated positive impact on social progress. The companies are listed in alphabetic order.

Type of CSR Initiatives	Companies
Cause promotion - fundraising, participation, or volunteer recruitment for a cause.	Tata
Cause Related Marketing - monetary or in-kind donations to product sales or other consumer action.	Whole Foods
Corporate Social Marketing - uses business resources to develop a behaviour change campaign intended to improve public health, safety, the environment, or community well-being.	Nestle, Unilever, Body Shop, Starbucks, Bat'a
Corporate Philanthropy - involves a corporation making a direct contribution to a charity, in the form of cash, donations, and in-kind services.	Facebook, Cobani, Microsoft
Employee Engagement - encourage employees to engage with non-profit organizations by volunteering their expertise, talents, ideas and labour.	IBM
Socially Responsible Business Practices - practices, not mandated by law that a corporation adopts to support social causes in order to improve community well-being and protect the environment by reducing, recycling or reusing.	BMW, Hilton, Nike

The family-owned global footwear company **Bat'a** had a strategy to set up villages around the factories and supply schools and welfare to improve the life of the community. At the core of Bata's philosophy was to keep the workforce happy and productive. These villages spread in several countries across the world including Netherlands, Slovakia, Czech Republic, Croatia, Switzerland, France, Canada, England, Pakistan and India and some of those factories are still active today. Founder Tomáš Bat'a was not only a successful entrepreneur and businessman creating one of the Czech Republic's most famous brands, but also a respected social innovator who was committed to improve the life of its workers and well-being of the community. [119]

BMW Group sees global sustainability challenges as an opportunity to develop innovative products and services. Within company strategy, innovations are developed to be of benefit to customers and also have a positive impact on society and the environment. BMW adopted General Assembly of the United Nations' Sustainable Development Goals (SDGs) as a framework to align corporate sustainability goals in such a way that they contribute towards solving global environmental and societal challenges. As a result, BMW continuously improves the environmental targets set in CO_2

emissions, usage of renewable raw materials, reduction of waste and usage of renewable energy sources.

Figure 4.1 – CO2 Emission and Waste for Disposal per Vehicle

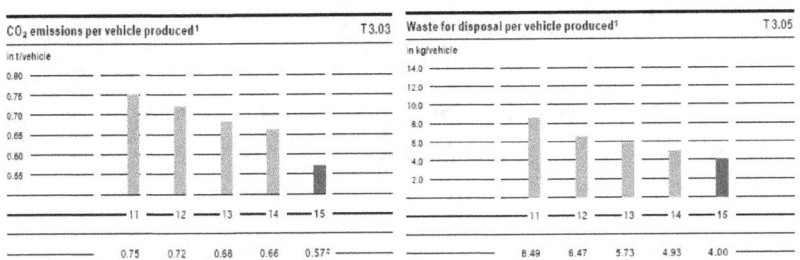

[58, pg.42,44]

BMW recycle 95% of materials in all vehicle models since 2008, meeting the requirements set for 2015. So, it is no surprise that BMW has reached the first place in the automotive industry on the Dow Jones Sustainability Indexes (DJSI) and reported as a top mark A in the CDP for climate protection measures sixth time a row, recognized as most sustainable premium car manufacturer. [58]

Another example of CSR initiative is the initiative "**Work Here**", which BMW launched in late 2015 in cooperation with the German Federal Employment Agency to help social integration. BMW offers qualified refugees the opportunity to take part in a nine-week course of practical training where the participants are accompanied by BMW employees as mentors and also receive language lessons and integration training [58, pg.76].

The **Body Shop** is regarded as a pioneer of modern corporate social responsibility as one of the first companies to publish a full report on its efforts and initiatives. Body Shop is guided by five core values; Activate Self Esteem, Against Animal Testing, Defend Human Rights, Protect Our Planet and Support Community Fair Trade. Launched 1987, **Community Fair Trade (CFT) program** helps marginalized communities improve their lives and alleviate poverty by trading fairly with suppliers. As part of this program, Body

Shop, <u>buys the finest ingredients and handcrafts directly from small-scale producers</u> around the world and in exchange, they offer them good trading practices and fair pricing. Over 90% of The Body Shop products contain community fair trade ingredients. [49]

In 2013, Body Shop spent over £9M on CFT ingredients working with 25 suppliers in 21 countries, directly helping to support 25,000 workers and benefiting 320,000 members of their wider communities. In the same year, Body Shop is rewarded with "International Business of 2013" prestigious honor.

Another example of philanthropic activity from a relatively small enterprise is done by **Cobani**, a New York based yogurt-maker. CEO and Founder of Cobani, Hamdi Ulukaya <u>gave its 2,000 employees 10% ownership of company's future value</u>. The goal, Ulukaya said, is to pass along the wealth they have helped build in the decade since the company started. Technology start-ups often pay employees partly in shares to help recruit them or to compete in a company's early days for in-demand workers, but this sort of transfer of shares is rare in the food industry. Ulukaya said "This isn't a gift. It is a mutual promise to work together with a shared purpose and responsibility. To continue to create something special and of lasting value." [28]

Facebook CEO Mark Zuckerberg and his wife Priscilla Chan announced that they will give away 99% of their Facebook stock, valued at around $45 billion, to the **Chan Zuckerberg Initiative**, a limited liability company the couple founded that will use the funds to promote "philanthropic, public advocacy, and other activities for the public good". This commitment is not only in line with the company's own CSR efforts but very positive to inspire millennial professionals to rethink charitable giving. [55]

In 2012, **Hilton** announced multi-year partnerships with Feeding America and The Global FoodBanking Network to secure food and reduce hunger in communities around the globe [54]. Roughly <u>one third of the food produced in the world for human consumption, gets wasted</u> each year. Food sent to landfills produces methane, a powerful greenhouse gas that contributes to global warming and climate change. According to the US Environmental Protection Agency, methane is 20 times more damaging to the environment than carbon dioxide. The collaborations will enable Hilton Worldwide hotels to collect safe, surplus food from conferences and daily food and beverage operations that would otherwise be thrown away and make it available to those in need. With this initiative, Hilton will turn an environmental problem into a humanitarian solution.

IBM's Corporate Service Corps program was launched in 2008 to help communities around the world solve critical problems. Corporate Service Corps selects top management volunteers and dispatches these leaders to emerging markets around the world to work on a variety of initiatives. Teams work collaboratively with local government and community counterparts to understand how to implement socially responsible business practices with measurable results in a global context. Since its launch in 2008, over 2500 employees have participated the program so far, helping over 140,000 people in 37 countries around the world and providing a triple benefit;

- Communities have their problems solved.
- IBMers receive leadership training and development.
- IBM develops new markets and global leaders.

As S. Litow, IBM's Vice President of Corporate Citizenship and Corporate Affairs stated "*It is not just philanthropy, it is leadership development and business development, and it helps build economic development in the emerging world. This allows us to build the experience and relevance to enter new markets.*" [57] Corporate Service Corps provides a triple benefit; communities have their problems solved, IBMers receive the leadership training and development, IBM develops new markets and global leaders [117].

Another program initiated by IBM is called **On Demand Community**. Launched in 2003, On Demand Community provides IBM employees and retirees with resources designed around specific opportunities such as project management, technology strategy and planning, disaster planning, science and math education to help them engage with community. Nearly 250,000 registered participants have collectively donated over 16 million hours in the program's first 10 years, to schools and not-for-profit organizations worldwide. [95]

IBM has been actively leading over a dozen of initiatives today covering a variety of areas from education, workforce development, environmental sustainability, economic development, healthcare to empower, improve and progress the society and make the world work better [120].

Microsoft has a mission to empower every person and every organization on the planet to achieve more in their communities by allowing them access to world-class productivity, platform and technologies. **Microsoft Philanthropies**, founded in 2016, creates a comprehensive and industry-leading donations program to provide cloud services to non-profit organizations worldwide. Microsoft will donate $1 billion in cloud services to non-profits and university researchers over the next three years with a goal to support 70,000 non-profits through this program. [60]

Nestlé looks at CSR in terms of creating shared value; business can help societies progress and all sectors can help business to improve and flourish. In 1962, Nestlé launched **Milk District** program in Northern district of Moga in India to support the economic development of dairy farmers. Till then, a dairy farmer typically owned less than five acres of poorly irrigated and infertile soil, many kept a single buffalo cow that produced just enough milk for their own and sixty percent of calves died new-born. Due to lack of refrigeration, milk could not travel far and was frequently contaminated. As part of Milk District program, Nestlé built refrigerated dairies as collection points for milk in each town and sent its trucks to the dairies with veterinarians and nutritionists to collect the milk. To help farmers improve milk productivity and quality, monthly technical field trainings were conducted, and regular audits were enforced to ensure that good farm practices were implemented. [30, pg.13]

42

Today, milk district model is operating in 31 countries and help about 352,000 dairy farmers who supply milk directly to factories. On an average Nestlé milk districts are growing 2% - 5% annually, and in some cases as high as 10%. The result is a <u>Win-Win situation for all</u>. Nestlé does not own any agricultural land or farms, but ensures a regular supply of high-quality fresh milk. Yet Nestlé is committed to develop long-term credible relationships with dairy farmers based on mutual trust. This makes mutual economic sense and ensures long-term sustainability. Farmers' income is increased, employment is generated for rural residents and significant improvements in the standards of living is achieved. [52, pg.12, 35]

Figure 4.2 – Nestle's Milk District Model

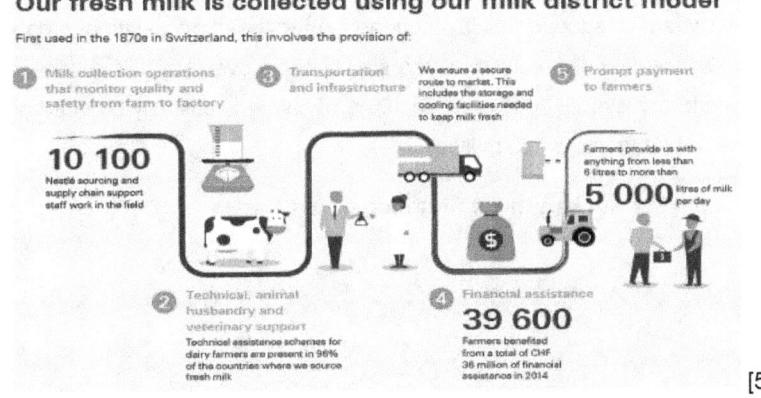

[53]

Nike's sustainable innovation, '**Color Dry**', is a great example of how revolutionary technologies can lead to bottom-line savings for company and also improve the water use and waste across the supply chain. The World Economic Forum has flagged water quantity and quality as the biggest threat facing the planet over the next decade. In order to reduce and improve water use in dyeing factories, Nike developed a new carbon-based dyeing process that eliminates water and chemical and uses recycled CO_2 instead. The savings are significant. Compared to traditional dyeing methods, the Color Dry process reduces dyeing time by 40 percent, energy use by around 60 percent. Through FY15, one facility produced 600,000 yards of fabric for Color Dry polos, saving 20 million liters of water. [92, pg.43] COO E. Sprunk said *"We see sustainability and business growth as complementary and our strategy is to prioritize relationships with factory groups that demonstrate a desire to invest in sustainable practices and technologies."* [93]

Starbucks launched **C.A.F.E.** (Coffee and Farmer Equity) practice in 2004 to ensure the company sources sustainably grown and processed coffee by evaluating the economic, social and environmental aspects of coffee production. The practice includes responsible purchasing practices, farmer support, economic, social and environmental standards for suppliers, industry collaboration and community development programs. As part of this program, Starbucks provided loans to farmers for tree renovation. Coffee trees don't produce forever and replacing old trees is needed to ensure a healthy crop year after year. To support this investment, farmers need access to affordable credit to assure a more resilient coffee supply chain over time. Starbucks put two goals to achieve by 2015; ensure 100% of coffee is ethically sourced and increase farmer loans to $20 million.

Figure 4.3 – Starbucks Ethical Sourcing Goal Charts

[84, pg.7]

Tata Sons Ltd., the holding company of the Tata Group, has been very committed in fulfilling its duty and responsibility towards the social development reaching the masses to improve their life standard and to exploit the employable skills. The Tata's credo is 'give back to the people what you have earned from them'. As stated by J. R. D. Tata, former chairman of Tata Sons, "*No success or achievement in material terms is worthwhile unless it serves the needs or interests of the country and its people.*" Tata Sons Ltd. utilizes on average between 8 to 14% of its net profit every year for various social causes (hospitals, sports academies, cultural centers, educational infrastructure, etc.) through the trusts endowed by members of the Tata family. [59]

Launched in 2010, the **Unilever Sustainable Living Plan** is blueprint for company's sustainable growth, with vision to grow business, and at the same time decouple environmental footprint from growth and increase positive social impact. The plan ensures that 100% of the materials used in Unilever's products are sustainable, and that all links along supply chains meet ethical, social and environmental values. Unilever has a simple but clear purpose; to make sustainable living commonplace. [pg.4]

In order to enhance the livelihoods of people in developing countries and particularly in support of women, Unilever launched **Project Shakti** in India in 2012. Instead of using its customary wholesaler-to-retailer distribution model to reach remote villages, Unilever recruited village women, provided them with access to microfinance loans, and trained them in selling soaps, detergents, and another products door-to-door. More than 65,000 women entrepreneurs now participate the program, nearly doubling their household incomes on average, while increasing rural access to hygiene products and thus contributing to public health. These social gains also led to business gains for the company. As of 2012 Project Shakti had achieved more than $100 million in sales. [32, pg.4]

Whole Foods is a dynamic leader in the quality food business. Whole Foods motto; 'Whole Foods, Whole People, Whole Planet', emphasizes that their vision reaches far beyond just being a food retailer, measuring customer satisfaction, team member happiness, return on capital investment, improvement in the state of the environment and local and larger community support. Whole Foods supports sustainable agriculture, promotes the reduction of waste and consumption of non-renewable resources. In order to support non-profits in local communities, Whole Foods stores hold "**Five percent days**" fundraising quarterly where five percent of store sales go to a local non-profit or educational organization. In 2012, Whole Foods Market stores raised a combined total of more than $5 million "five percent days". [54]

Chapter 5 - Leadership's pivotal role in CSR programs

In this chapter, I will review the literature on leadership theories and explore the link between leadership and corporate responsibility.

Leadership has been a hot topic for many researchers. The search scope spans from political leaders to business leaders covering various models and practices including transformational leadership, charismatic leadership and visionary leadership. S. J. Zaccaro, C. Kemp, P. Bader (2003) has conducted a detailed search on leadership outcomes examining studies published over a decade that have received substantial empirical support. As a summary of their research, they categorized **leadership attributes** in six groups [105, pg.18]:

1. Cognitive capacities - General intelligence, creative thinking capacities
2. Personality – Extroversion, conscientiousness, emotional stability, openness, agreeableness
3. Motives and needs - Need for power, need for achievement, motivation to lead
4. Social capacities – Self-monitoring, social intelligence, emotional intelligence
5. Problem-solving skills – Problem construction, solution generation
6. Tacit knowledge

Over the time, a number of leadership theories have been evolved. The most popular ones are:

- Trait theory- Identifies the specific personality traits that distinguish leaders from non-leaders.´ Based on the premise that **leaders are 'born, not made'**, that leadership is largely innate, rather than being developed through learning [104]. The personal traits of goods leaders can be summarized as inner motivation, adaptability, open-mindedness, self-confidence, vision, intelligence, knowledge and desire to lead.

- Behavioral theory – Assumes that leadership capability can be learned, rather than being inherent. Successful leadership is based in definable, learnable behavior.

- Contingency theory – Assumes that leader's ability to lead is contingent upon various situational factors and there no single optimal profile of a leader exists.

- Transactional theory – Known also as **managerial leadership**, the leader's main focus is supervising and ensuring that things are done rather than transforming or improving the future. The team is motivated by reward and punishment.

- Transformational theory – Defined as a leadership approach that causes change in individuals and social systems. Enhances the motivation, morale and performance of followers through a variety of mechanisms. In its ideal form, it creates valuable and positive change in the followers with the end goal of developing followers into leaders.

In order to examine the link between leadership and corporate responsibility, D. Mazutis & C. Zintel (2014) conducted a comprehensive review of all published quantitative studies between 1976 and 2014 and introduced a model, in which several dimensions of leadership are identified that relate either directly or indirectly to corporate responsibility processes. The summary of their findings is enclosed.

Figure 5.1 – Leadership Dimensions in Relation to Corporate Responsibility

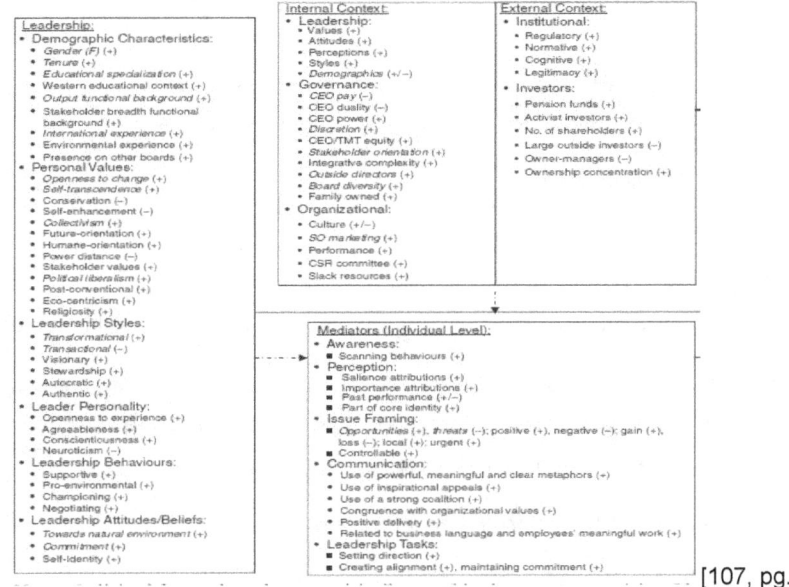

[107, pg.9]

Mirvis and Googins (2006) developed a framework describing various stages of corporate citizenship, starting from elementary stage to all the way to transforming stage where the contribution of leadership scales between lack of interest to a more visionary level that they drive the vision and set the organizational structure.

Figure 5.2 – Stages of Corporate Citizenship

Dimensions		Stage 1: Elementary	Stage 2: Engaged	Stage 3: Innovative	Stage 4: Integrated	Stage 5: Transforming
	Citizenship Concept	Jobs, Profits & Taxes	Philanthropy, Environmental Protection	Stakeholder Management	Sustainability or Triple Bottom Line	Change the Game
	Strategic Intent	Legal Compliance	License to Operate	Business Case	Value Proposition	Market Creation or Social Change
	Leadership	Lip Service, Out of Touch	Supporter, In the Loop	Steward, On Top of It	Champion, In Front of It	Visionary, Ahead of the Pack
	Structure	Marginal: Staff Driven	Functional Ownership	Cross-Functional Coordination	Organizational Alignment	Mainstream: Business Driven
	Issues Management	Defensive	Reactive, Policies	Responsive, Pro-Active, Programs	Pro-Active, Systems	Defining
	Stakeholder Relationships	Unilateral	Interactive	Mutual Partnership Influence	Alliance	Multi-Organization
	Transparency	Flank Protection	Public Relations	Public Reporting	Assurance	Full Disclosure

[111, pg.5]

In a different study, Tulder and Zwart (2006) defined four different types of leadership relate to different approaches towards corporate responsibility. Their findings are summarized in the table below;

Figure 5.3 – Four CSR Approaches & Leadership

IN-ACTIVE	RE-ACTIVE	ACTIVE	PRO/INTER-ACTIVE
"Corporate *Self* Responsibility"	"Corporate Social *Responsiveness*"	"Corporate Social Responsibility"	"Corporate *Societal* Responsibility"
Inside-in	Outside-in	Inside-out	In/outside-in/out
"doing things right"	"don't do things wrong'	'doing the right things'	"doing the right things right'
Efficiency		Equity/Ethics	Effectiveness
Transactional and team leaders	Charismatic leaders	Visionary and moral leaders	Transformational leaders
Utilitarian motive: Profit maximisation	Negative duty approach: Quarterly profits and market capitalisation	'Positive duty' or 'virtue based': Values (long-term profitability)	Interactive duty approach: Medium-term profitability and sustainability
'trust me'		'proof it to me'	'involve/engage me'; 'join me'
Economic Responsibility [Wealth oriented] Narrow (internal) CSR	←	→	*Social Responsibility* [welfare oriented] Broad (external) CSR

[76]

According to their study, **"Visionary" and "Moral" leadership** both require an idea/vision of where the organization should be in the future and visionary leadership in particular can be considered as a precondition for

50

'transformational leadership'. Transformational leadership, on the other hand, is the most outward oriented type of leadership and directed at formulating and implementing a new organizational vision that is embedded in a broader vision of society and the active involvement of external stakeholders. The key to real transformational leadership lies in the effectiveness of their action.

Ethical leadership and responsible leadership are also contemporary developments in the leadership literature, where the concepts of ethnical leadership and CSR values have similarities. Maak & Pless (2006) defined responsible leaders as responsible individuals who live by values and principles and have potential for contributing to the betterment of the society and developed a roles model.

Figure 5.4 – The Role Model of Responsible Leadership

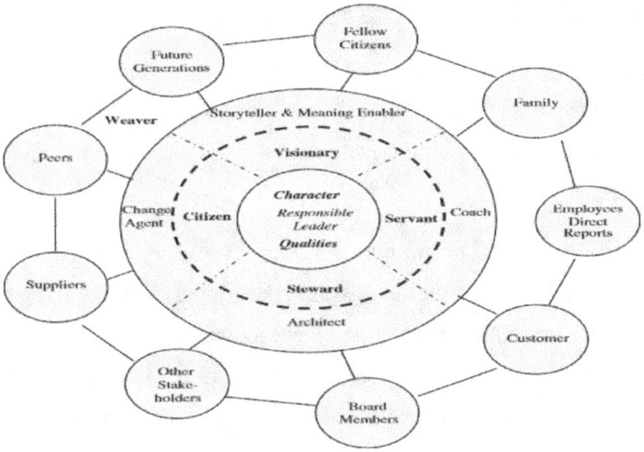

[112, pg.9]

According to Bass & Steidelmeier (1999), the ultimate goal of ethical leadership is to achieve a common good such as business sustainability and organizational legitimacy [113].

As discussed in the previous chapters, when it comes to CSR, there are no easy answers on what to do or how to do it. A company's interactions and interdependencies with society are many and complex [79]. Leaders must manage a broad array of activities and goals. It is accepted that different styles of leadership may work better in different cultures, and the same approach may not work for every CSR initiative within the same company. Time to time companies have to adjust their strategies to keep up with changes. But one thing is clear that without active and effective of leadership at a political, institutional and individual level, CSR initiatives will fall short to deliver the value they promise.

Individual and organizational leadership plays a key role in initiating, promoting and executing CSR programs. As we discussed in Chapter 2, the positive outcome of any CSR project largely depends on employee motivation and commitment. Employees first need to be motivated to carry on any CSR requirements and then be committed to deliver. It is leaders' job to set direction, create alignment, and maintain commitment within the organization. Leadership is a key element in any successful CSR program.

The biggest challenge in the field of CSR implementation is the development of leaders, looking for what kind of leader is needed for building a sustainable global society and how we can best develop individuals with these leadership capabilities [21, pg.8].

Another challenge is, CSR programs are often initiated and run in an uncoordinated way by a variety of managers, frequently without the active engagement of CEO and often there is no single executive in charge of these programs [32, pg.3]. When leaders aren't engaged and the strategy about corporate citizenship is not embraced broadly, program tends to have limited life and impact.

Kakabadse (2007) identified three stages of CSR implementation where specific leadership capabilities are needed. These are decision-making stage, which includes the leadership capabilities of awareness, reflexivity, and CSR goal discerning; adoption stage, which includes the leadership capabilities of using business case language, persuasion, handle conflicting priorities and CSR measurement, and commitment stage which includes will to act. [81, pg.2]

As shown in the figure below, the skills are interconnected, in the sense that all need to be employed at many points over the course of time, and in that they need to be often used together to face inevitable challenges confronting the implementation of CSR.

Figure 5.5 – CSR Leaders Roadmap

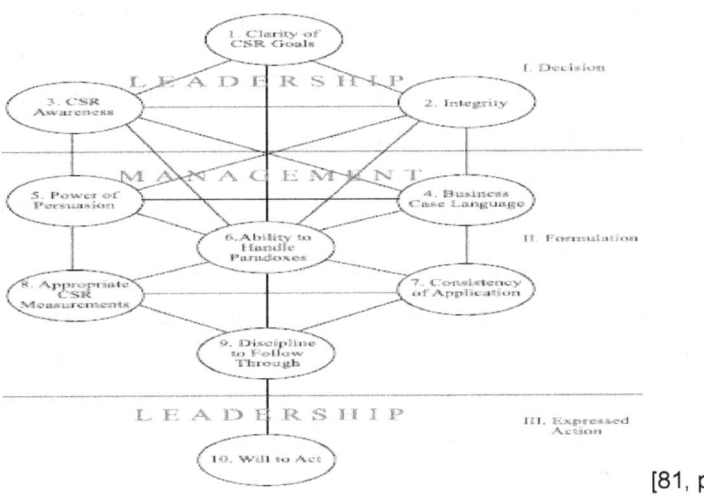

[81, pg.6]

Visser (2001) summarized key characteristics of CSR leadership as having systemic and interdisciplinary understanding, emotional intelligence and caring attitude, value orientation that shapes culture, compelling vision for making a difference, inclusive style that engenders trust, innovative approach, and long-term perspective. [77, pg.3] Bass (1985) defined superior leadership performance when leaders broaden and elevate the interests of their employees, when they generate awareness and acceptance of the purposes and mission of the group, and when they stir their employees to look beyond their own self-interest for the good of the group [106, pg.21]. A CSR leader is someone who inspires and supports action towards a better world.

A good example of CSR leadership is Wells Fargo's approach, where the culture of leadership and community engagement is embedded throughout the company's culture. CEO J. Stumpf says *"We expect all of our team members to be community leaders. We need all of them, regardless of rank or title, to be our eyes and ears, to help us identify and decide how Wells Fargo should respond to community needs."* Members of the operating committee meet regularly with stakeholders to listen and understand their concerns and Board of Directors holds the company's leaders accountable for progress. [80]

Another good example is IBM's approach to CSR. *"IBM thinks of it as a growth strategy. Our corporate responsibility and philanthropic activities are deeply connected to our core values."* says S. Litow, IBM's Vice President of Corporate Citizenship and Corporate Affairs. Since he joined IBM in 1993, he was part of several transformation both in the IT market and the company's history, yet IBM's approach and commitment to CSR has not changed. [82]

Salesforce's "1-1-1" model to integrate CSR into organization is also very effective. The model suggests that 1% of the founding stock goes to the corporate foundation to help communities in need; employees are paid to donate 1% of their time to activities that fit with the philanthropic priorities of the company; and 1% of customer subscriptions are donated to nonprofits to increase their operating effectiveness [110, pg.2].

Bold actions by global leaders such as P. Polman, CEO of Unilever, have a ripple effect in the market. Polman became an exemplar in his break-through thinking when he came on board in 2009. One of his first actions was to stop issuing quarterly investor guidance and earnings targets. Polman points out that the average tenure of a CEO is only three years so there is often little motivation to take on the challenge. Yet, by taking a long-term perspective and shunning quarterly demands, companies can make decisions that ensure the continuing viability and profitability of the business. [89]

Other well-known examples of leaders who prioritized CSR-driven strategies include Anita Roddick who developed at Body Shop a new product category on non-animal testing procedures, Ben Cohen who supported local business at Ben and Jerry's, Paul Newman who differentiated its brand with donations

[108, pg.3] and Tomáš Baťa who inspired the world by setting up villages around the factories and supplying schools and welfare to improve the life of the community.

As a summary, being a CSR leader is more than wanting to help the planet [81, pg.1]. Leader are accountable for corporate's sustainability strategy and face the big challenge of preparing their organization in implementing the CSR vision. Lagging in leadership will diminish the effect of CSR initiatives and may turn CSR to become a costly exercise in public relations. Companies having visionary and transformation leaders in place, or managed by ethical and responsible leaders have a leapfrog advantage in putting the right CSR strategy in action to contribute to the well-being of the society and as well differentiating themselves from their competitors.

In the scope of this study, I took the transformational leadership, proposed by Burns (Burns, 1978) and further developed Bass and Avolio (Bass & Avolio, 2000) as the basic model for two fundamental reasons. First, transformational leadership has been seen as one of the most effective theories for companies driving higher performance. Second, transformational leadership inspires more institutional CSR practices. Also, my analysis on leadership is in the context of stakeholder theory which suggests that business is composed of various stakeholders all of whom have a legitimate strategic and moral stake in the organization, and business is not only responsible for their economic bottom-line, but also responsible for the well-being of society and the state of the environment. It is also recommended to conduct a further study on the new emerging types of business leaders, called social entrepreneurs, who have characteristics of a high-level of empathy and need for social justice that distinguishes them from commercial counterparts. [100, pg.599]

Can companies do well by doing good?

Part III – CSR

Key Issues &

Debates

Can companies do well by doing good?

Chapter 6 - Can social performance be measured?

Measuring social performance remains as one of the greatest mystery in CSR domain. One of the key reason is, social performance is multi-dimensional and spans numerous social and environmental issues [51, pg.170]. What methods to use, what metrics to choose from (whether qualitative or quantitative) and the range of social benefits to be captured over time remains as the key challenges [19, pg.403]. The scope and focus of CSR initiatives are most of the time unique for each organization and this makes it even more difficult to establish universal codes of conduct. Social and business benefits are often long-term or intangible, which make systematic measurement more complex [11, pg.4]. Today, most companies measure progress in CSR by assessing progress towards meeting internal CSR targets year on year [19, pg.403].

The financial measures can theoretically be categorized into two groups; accounting-based measures of financial returns (e.g., profitability, revenue, return on assets, return on equity) versus market-based measures of financial value (e.g., stock price, price-to-book ratio) [36, pg.13]. Accounting-based measures usually produce more positive results than market-based measures. Firms that have a better financial status are more likely to do some "window dressing" of their accounting data. On the other hand, the markets cannot be (especially under strong assumptions concerning their degree of efficiency) manipulated by the window dressing of accounting data or by any CSR ingratiating attempts [51, pg.58].

At present, there are no widely adopted methodologies to measure social value creation. The two classical evaluation methods are **cost-effectiveness analysis and cost benefit analysis**. Cost-effectiveness analysis involves the calculation of a ratio of cost to a non-monetary benefit or outcome. The problem with this approach is the ambiguity and amount of subjectivity involved in assigning a monetary value to an intangible item projected to be realized over a period of time in future. Cost-benefit analysis monetizes the benefits and costs associated with an intervention and then compares them to see which one is greater. Examples are net present value (NPV), benefit-cost ratios or the internal rate of return. The shortcoming of this approach is that it is highly demanding to gather data across various dimensions of social benefit accruing to various stakeholders [38, pg.10].

The other common methods to mention is SROI and IRIS. **Social Return on Investment (SROI)** provides a framework, a guideline for measuring, managing and accounting for social value or social impact [41]. An SROI ratio of 2:1 means that for every $1 invested in the organization, $2 of social value are generated [39, pg.16]. There is no clear suggestion though to the actual measurement of external costs and benefits. **Impact Reporting and Investing Standards (IRIS)**, an initiative of the Global Impact Investing Network, is the catalogue of generally-accepted performance metrics to measure social, environmental, and financial performance [40].

Researchers acknowledged a number of weaknesses in these methodologies such as there is wide variation in how companies are assessed on their corporate social performance, there is lack of transparency of audit process, and much of the business value contributing to the intangibles, which may show up in profits several years later [11, pg.54]. **There is no single "silver bullet"** impact measurement framework or methodology that can be applied to all organizations [39, pg.5]. As a result, measures of corporate social performance vary widely and tend to capture either a single specific dimension, such as philanthropic contributions or pollution control, or broad appraisals of corporate social performance as a whole. [36, pg.7].

There are a variety of CSR measurement tools developed today that companies can leverage to measure their CSR performance. Those tools range from being performance benchmarking and ranking tools such as Dow Jones Sustainability Index, certification and accreditation standards such as ISO14001 and SA8000, reporting guidelines such as the Global Reporting Initiative (GRI) and UN Global Compact principles. OECD in its 2008's Annual Report, classified CSR instruments for multinational enterprises in three categories.

Figure 6.1 – Classification of CSR Instruments

Instrument and Role	Examples
International Conventions and Declarations. • Reflect agreed international normative principles. Directed mainly to government for domestic implementation. These can help business understand *what* to do.	Universal Declaration of Human Rights. UN Framework Convention on Climate Change. ILO Conventions. ILO Declaration on Fundamental Principles and Rights at Work. UN Millennium Development Goals. World Summit on Sustainable Development Plan of Implementation. OECD Convention on Combating Bribery of Foreign Officials in International Business Transactions.
Officially-agreed or recognised guidance. • Offer authoritative guidance to the business sector on expectations of behaviour. Also help understand *what* to do, and sometimes also *how*.	ILO MNE Declaration. OECD MNE Guidelines. UN Global Compact Principles. International Finance Corporation Performance Standards. Extractive Industries Transparency Initiative (EITI) Principles.
Privately developed principles. • Offer business/civil society developed guidance on expectations of behaviour. These sometimes also provide guidance on *how* to implement such standards. These may or may not be derived from international norms.	ISO standards (*e.g.* 14000 series). GRI Sustainability Reporting Guidelines. Responsible Care Guidelines. ICMM Sustainable Development Principles. Electronic Industry Code of Conduct.

[115, pg.6]

A selective review of the internationally-accepted frameworks, guidelines, indices, ratings is summarized in "Appendix A".

There arises some skepticism on CSR reporting efforts, where in many occasions, companies tend to use CSR reports to demonstrate to stakeholders that the company is managing its societal impacts responsibly, rather than proactively investing in it to generate returns for society and shareholders. Yet, <u>CSR reporting has become a mainstream practice for many companies</u>. According to an international study by KPMG [2], 95% of the world's largest 250 companies publish annual sustainability reports.

A CSR report is a non-financial document focusing on three areas [5];

- Environmental - the company's impact on the environment, which includes energy and water consumption reduction efforts, waste recycling efforts
- Social - the company's impact in society, which includes its charitable contributions, employee volunteerism, workplace safety, diversity, human rights
- Governance and ethics - the company's governance practices and policies, management structure, data privacy and compliance practices

As a summary, measuring social performance is a **challenging task**. CSR environment is constantly changing, and the existing international systems and indices are continuously being refined. There is **no one common method or tool that can be broadly endorsed** to measure the impact of CSR initiatives on social performance for companies of all sizes and industries. The results can be misleading due to ambiguity and amount of subjectivity in data collection, realization of intangible benefits in the foreseen future, and lack of transparency of the audit process. Despite all the challenges and issues along, CSR reporting has become a mainstream practice and companies leverage internationally-accepted frameworks, guidelines to evaluate and benchmark their CSR performance.

Chapter 7 - Is CSR good for firm's financial performance?

As discussed in the earlier chapters, the CSR initiatives can contribute to business many ways, but they often come at a cost. A considerable amount of research has focused on to find if there is a win-win situation, where being a good corporate citizen can also make a firm more profitable and whether these costs can be offset by direct economic or competitive benefits to the business, or by a premium in its stock price [46, pg.9]. The most proven financial benefits of effective strategic CSR are found in the areas of human resources and talent management, reputation and branding, and operational cost savings [7, pg.2].

There are two sides of debates concerning the CSR; shareholder theory and stakeholder theory. The advocates of the shareholder theory claim that companies are business entities with essential goal to create wealth and contribute to material well-being of its shareholders. The advocates of the stakeholder theory claim that the mission to distribute wealth equally, endorse human rights or repair the natural environment are the pillars of corporate's foundation.

The supporters of shareholder theory criticize companies using the CSR concept as a PR tool, simply for reputation building. Visser (2011) takes even a more cynical view suggesting that the incremental approach to CSR simply does not produce the scale and urgency of response that is required [94, pg.5]. According to him, the markets are designed to serve the financial and economic interests of the powerful, not the idealistic dreams of CSR advocates or the angry demands of civil society activists [94, pg.6]. Yet, supporters of stakeholder theory believe that without any social purpose, company's existence would be disruptive, and this is against the basic principle of societal development.

I'd agree with some of the opposing arguments that companies investing in CSR with simple motive of increasing their profitability are doomed to fail. Companies have resources, but they are not infinite. As the profits begin to disappear, CSR projects happen to be the first ones put on the shelf or reduced in scope.

I'd also agree that companies that initiate CSR simply for moral purposes would lose their power as soon as the moral component, mostly coming from the owner, cease to exist. On the similar lines, CSR that are put in practice only to comply with legal/governmental requirements and/or respond to media, would be short-sighted projects and will not go beyond being a soft contributor to general problems.

In my view, in alignment with the findings of the study done Z. Cheers (2011) both the stakeholder and shareholder theories alone are not complete. Companies should maximize long-term shareholder wealth, but not at the expense of stakeholders and ethical guidelines. Companies cannot be profitable in the long term if they have poor relations with their stakeholders. At the same time, companies cannot meet all the needs of their stakeholders and remain profitable. [85, pg.29]

In this chapter, I will explore if there is a correlation between Corporate Social Performance (CSP) and Corporate Financial Performance (CFP) and if companies can do well by doing good. This is for sure not a simple equation as factors such as company culture, company size, industry, leadership team and CRS activities selected alone may have an influence. A. Savitz calls this 'sweet-spot' where a company can meet its business objectives and as well the needs of the society or the environment at the same time [99].

Audrey Choi, CEO of Morgan Stanley's Institute for Sustainable Investing, stated in one of her public speech at TED conference that companies invested in sustainability outperforms their rivals by better operational efficiency, lower cost of capital and better performance in their stock price. According to her, they didn't make that outperformance by giving away money but focusing on the things that matter to their business, like wasting less energy; like making sure CEOs incentivized for the long-term results of the company, but not just quarterly results; or building a first-class culture that would have higher employee loyalty, retention and productivity. [65]

Margolis & Walsh (2003) assessed 127 empirical studies exploring the relationship of Corporate Social Performance and Corporate Financial Performance. They came to the conclusion that there are more findings suggesting a positive link, and only very little evidence of negative associations. There are some cases that it has not been possible to determine whether the association is either positive or negative. Orlitzky, Schmidt & Rynes (2003) carried out a meta-analysis of 52 studies assessing the relationship, which gave more detailed insights into the positive link based on the fact that CSP helps companies to build a positive reputation and goodwill with its external stakeholders. Another conclusion of the study was that, CSP is more highly correlated with accounting-based measures of CFP than with market-based indicators. [3, pg.13].

The results of another meta-analyses of 167 studies done by Harvard Business School, University of California and University of Michigan to explore the association between corporate social performance and corporate financial performance, concluded that there is a mildly positive relationship between CSR and corporate financial performance and finds no indication that corporate social investments systematically decrease shareholder value [11, pg.54].

Reviewing the findings of major studies referenced above, we can conclude that there is a positive link between CSP and CFP. It is also important to analyze whether CSR is observable in the short-term or long-term and whether it is applicable to all industries and company sizes.

First of all, CSR is a long-term commitment and it does not show quarterly results. Many research studies have proven that practicing CSR actually benefits companies significantly when they implement it effectively in the long term [23, pg.7]. McKinsey conducted a survey asking CFOs and investment professionals around the world to identify whether environmental, social, and governance programs create value. Respondents largely agreed that environmental and social programs will create value over the long term, and that governance programs create value in both the short and long terms [79]

Figure 7.1 – McKinsey Survey on Long-term Contribution to Shareholder value

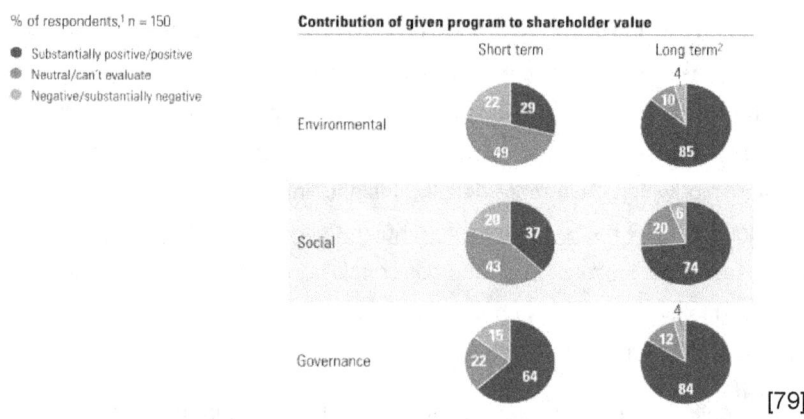

[79]

Secondly, a joint research done by University of New York and University of Texas in 2009, collecting a large dataset of charitable contributions made by public companies from 1989 through 2000 in US and applying Granger causality statistical methodology, revealed that charitable contributions increased the subsequent revenue growth of their donors. Yet, this causal relationship was found only in industries highly sensitive to consumer perception. A similar study done by Columbia Business School and Wharton School found a positive relationship between philanthropy and company financial performance in advertising-intensive industries, such as consumer-oriented companies. According to Servaes & Tamayo (2013), for firms with low public awareness, the impact of corporate social responsibility activities on firm value is either insignificant or negative [61, pg.3].

US Chamber of Commerce Foundation undertook a study to analyze the impact of CSR activities on the business sentiments of leading organizations across four industries. The analysis is based on data extracted from the sources covering news, blogs, message boards, reviews sites and Twitter, for the time period 28th February 2015 to 17th March 2015. The findings of the study were Information (58%) has the highest share of buzz and the highest share in CSR activities (51%) across other industries. With respect to the sentiment analysis, the Finance & Insurance sector has the highest positive sentiment, where the Retail sector has the highest negative view.

Figure 7.2 – US Chamber of Commerce Study on CSR

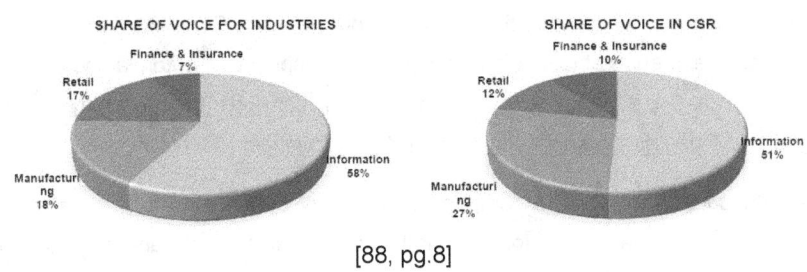

[88, pg.8]

As a third point, according to the results of the study done to measure the potential effects of company's age and size on the level of CSR, company size is found to be a significant determinant of CSR causing a U-shaped effect. This U-shaped effect of company size implies that the level of CSR activities decreases as a company grows from small to middle-sized but increases from middle-sized to large company.

Figure 7.3 – U-shaped Pattern of Sustainability Score

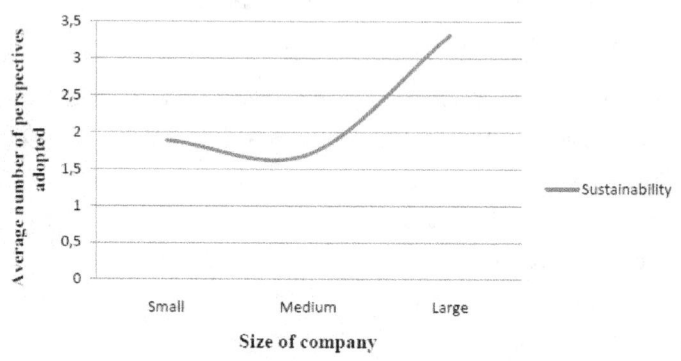

[4, pg.45]

A study commissioned by Danish Ministry of Economic and Business Affairs to determine whether any measurable economic or competitive benefits can result from the CSR activities of the small and medium sized enterprises (SMEs) in Denmark, suggests that some, but not all, CSR activities of SMEs can create measurable economic benefits. Despite the potential economic benefits, it is clear that many companies still <u>cannot measure or track the costs and benefits associated with their CSR activities</u>. [46, pg.39]

Also according to KPMG a company's most significant CSR impacts are often found not in its own operations, but in its value chain – upstream in the social and environmental impacts of its suppliers, and downstream in the impacts of its products and services through use and disposal [2, pg.62].

As a last point, I'd like to highlight some metrics that are used to evaluate companies' social performance. One of the common metrics is the stock price. Research by Bob Eccles and George Serafeim of Harvard Business School has shown that investments in <u>purpose-driven companies outperformed more traditional investments in the long run</u>. Their analysis revealed that a dollar invested in the value-weighted portfolio of a "high-sustainability firm" in 1993 would have been worth $22.60 by 2010, versus only $15.40 for a dollar invested in a more traditional firm. [10, pg. 7]

Although, a firms' reputation is an intangible asset and it is difficult to formulate how it can contribute to firm's overall performance, there are empirical studies to show that CSR affects firm's performance through the development of better relationships with customers/consumers. As an example, based on the search done by Reputation Institute on "Return on Reputation", reputable firms perform better recovery after crisis and take the advantage of benefit of doubt, 54% versus 20% in comparison to less reputable companies in a crisis [24, pg.12]. The chart shows the RepTrak® Portfolio has outperformed the S&P500 Index since 2006.

Figure 7.4 – Reputation Institute Analysis on Reputation and Stock Value

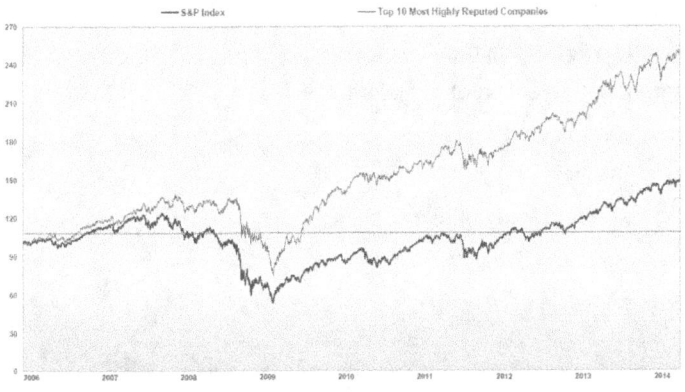

[24, pg.20]

Nielsen reviewed retail sales data across 20 brands in nine countries. These brands either included sustainability claims on packaging or actively promoted their sustainability actions through marketing efforts. The results from a March 2014 year-over-year analysis show an average annual sales increase of two percent for products with sustainability claims on the packaging and a lift of five percent for products that promoted sustainability actions through marketing programs. A review of 14 other brands without sustainability claims or marketing shows a sales rise of only one percent. [24, pg.5]

The conclusion that can be drawn from this section is that, there is a **positive relationship between** Corporate Social Performance and Corporate

Financial Performance, and CSR **can positively affect firm's value** when the initiatives are correctly aligned with business objectives. Yet, CSR does not show quarterly results. The financial gain is <u>observed in the long run</u> and it is more effective in <u>consumer-oriented industries</u>. <u>Company size</u> is also a significant determinant of CSR's effectiveness. Companies with higher reputation of sustainability tend to perform better in stock evaluation and have better sales ratio in comparison to others.

Areas where CSR can enhance firm's performance are summarized below;

- enhanced corporate image and brand reputation
- improved customer loyalty
- increased sales and market share
- higher employee engagement
- recruitment and retention of top talent
- decreased operational costs
- appeal to investors
- creating competitive advantage

Chapter 8 – Do Consumers Care about CSR?

The key question is if consumers care about CSR and if yes, then if CSR initiatives can have an impact on their purchasing decisions. In their study, S. Wu and H. Lin (2014) explored the same question from academic perspective and analyzed if the four dimensions proposed by Carroll (economic, legal, ethical, and philanthropic responsibilities) impact the brand trust, the brand satisfaction, and the brand attachment and whether they have any correlation with consumer's current purchasing behavior and future purchase intention. They concluded that ethical responsibility and brand satisfaction exhibited the strongest correlation. [83]

Figure 8.1 – Research Framework

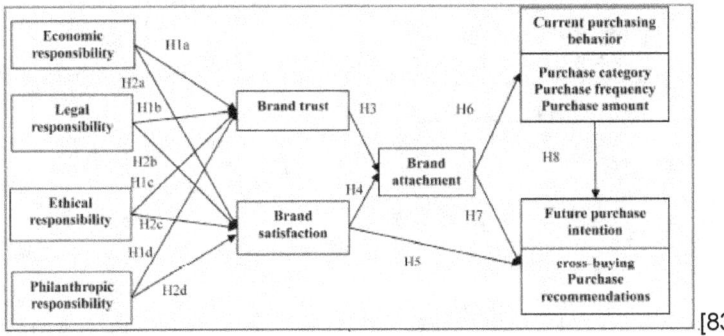

[83, pg.5]

Studies have shown that consumers generally value ethical products and are more likely to purchase a product if they perceive the company that makes it as socially responsible. Though, many do not like to pay a premium or sacrifice quality. A key finding from a study conducted by Cause Marketing

Forum in 2014, reveals that the vast majority (84%) of consumers claim they would likely switch brands to one affiliated with a good cause if price and quality were similar [12]. Another study done by Cone Communications in 2013, 91% of global consumers are likely to switch brands to one associated with a good cause, given comparable price and quality [13, pg.19].

Yet, in other studies, a positive trade-off between ethical and functional attributes is captured where consumers demonstrated marginal willingness to pay for social attributes. According to Nielsen 2014 Global Survey on CSR, polling 30,000 consumers in 60 countries, 55% of global online consumers responded that consumers are willing to pay more for products and services provided by companies that are committed to positive social and environmental impact. More than half of global respondents 52% of respondents say their purchase decisions are partly dependent on the packaging – they check the labelling first before buying to ensure the brand is committed to positive social and environmental impact. Millennials (age 21-34) appear more responsive to sustainability actions.

Figure 8.2 – Research Results on Consumers

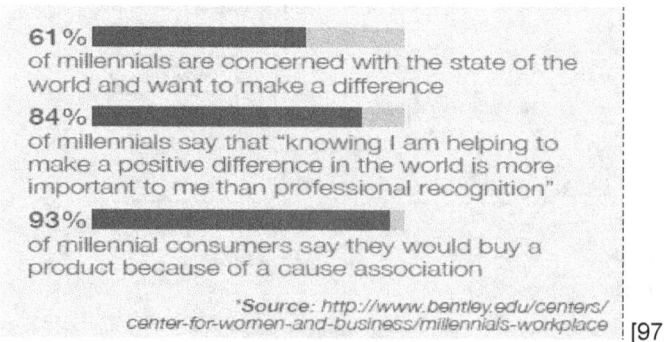

61% of millennials are concerned with the state of the world and want to make a difference

84% of millennials say that "knowing I am helping to make a positive difference in the world is more important to me than professional recognition"

93% of millennial consumers say they would buy a product because of a cause association

Source: http://www.bentley.edu/centers/ center-for-women-and-business/millennials-workplace [97, pg.4]

As consumers are getting more informed, selective and conscious thru the internet and social media about the products they purchase, the popularity of **ethical consumerism** is on the rise. *"Consumers around the world are saying* *loud and clear that a brand's social purpose is among the factors that influence purchase decisions"* said Amy Fenton, global leader of public development and sustainability for Nielsen [27]. Many surveys support that even the average consumer is demanding so-called ethical products, fair labor certified garments, cosmetics produced without animal testing, and products made through the use of sustainable technologies. However, when companies offer such products and/or services, the **buying behavior of consumers is often inconsistent,** and the percentage of shopping choices made on a truly ethical basis proved to be much smaller. [68] Although consumers respond positively about CSR, they still base their purchasing on traditional criteria such as price, quality, and convenience.

A study done to explore buying process of consumers related to consumer technology products in the UK, revealed that consumers struggled to translate their concern into green purchases. The finding was that the consumer behavior was complex and not all consumers reacted in the same way to certain CSR programs. The actual purchase <u>behavior forms only 4–10% of different product ranges although 30% of them reported</u> that they were very concerned about environmental issues. [45, pg.22]

According to Brinkmann & Peattie (2008), the reason why the buying behavior of consumers is often inconsistent to what they communicate at surveys is, <u>consumers are largely amoral, self-interested, rational-economically motivated individuals, with no responsibilities other than to meet their own needs</u>. 'Ethical consumer' is as an exceptional or abnormal specific sub-type of consumers. [69, pg.4] Consumers evaluate any CSR actions of a firm relative to their own personal morals, values, and priorities and social responsibility issues are not top criteria for many. <u>Free-riding</u> behavior, means enjoying the benefits of goods without paying, is another barrier [67, pg.5].

Another reason for consumer's inconsistent behavior is their lack of awareness of the company's CSR records and inconvenience of obtaining information to be able to judge if the product is ethically produced or not. Consumers tend to follow the path of least resistance, known as **principle of**

least effort, in their purchase behavior, minimizing search effort and maximizing convenience. A study conducted by Mohr (2001) revealed that, it is difficult for many respondents to use CSR in their buying decisions because they do not have enough information on what companies are doing, and they would have to work too hard to get it. Many respondents would like to have systematic information on companies' social responsibility records. [71] But they don't want to be pushed either and want to receive the information within their own initiatives. [73, pg.82] (Besides, many companies are not consistently responsible or irresponsible. Therefore, consumers would not know which firms to purchase from.)

Simon (1995) pointed out that while consumers have become quite receptive to corporate philanthropy, they are insufficiently informed about its actual practice by specific firms. It is important for communication strategies to be reassessed to increase the awareness levels among consumers, so they know which firms operate with CSR perspectives. [72]

As an example, 'being green' needs time and space in peoples' lives that is not available in increasingly busy lifestyles. Green consumers can use their buying power to make a difference, but at a high-cost in terms of effort and time, which is a significant barrier. These consumers need help from government in the form of incentives and single-issue labels to show them where they should be concentrating their limited efforts. [45, pg.32] A survey conducted over 43,000 Americans by JUST Capital in 2015 proved this point. According to survey results illustrated below, the vast majority of respondents said they would buy differently if they knew whether products were made by responsible companies.

Figure 8.3 – Survey of Corporate America

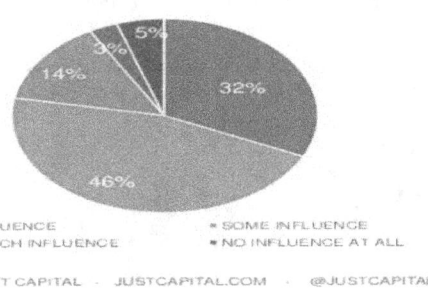

[66, Slide 7]

In order to better understand the factors that affect how CSR activities translate into consumer purchases, we need to analyze the <u>three value drivers; emotional, social, and functional</u>. Emotional value is received when a consumer makes a purchase with a social or environmental attribute (e.g. donations to charity). Social value can accrue from purchases from firms active in CSR since people make judgments about others based on the purchases they make. Consumers give lower priority to forms of CSR that generate emotional value and social value. On the other token, functional value relates to the actual benefit the consumer receives from the product or service. <u>Functional value is the leading and, in many cases, the sole driver</u>. **Consumers only support firms that engage in CSR if they receive some kind of value from the exchange**. [70]

As an example, consumers buy organics foods because they perceive them to be healthier and more nutritious. Consumers buy energy efficient cars because fuel efficiency standards save the environment, but after a few years, it saves them money. Sen and Bhattacharya (2001) also found that consumers are <u>more sensitive to negative CSR information than positive CSR information</u>. More specifically, all consumers react negatively to negative CSR information whereas only those who are most supportive to CSR issues react positively to positive CSR Information. [74, pg.15] Consumers are more likely to boycott irresponsible companies than to support responsible companies.

Based on the results of global CSR study conducted by Cone Communication in 2013, the economic development and environmental issues are the most pressing issue consumers want companies to address.

Figure 8.4 – Issues Consumer want Companies to Address

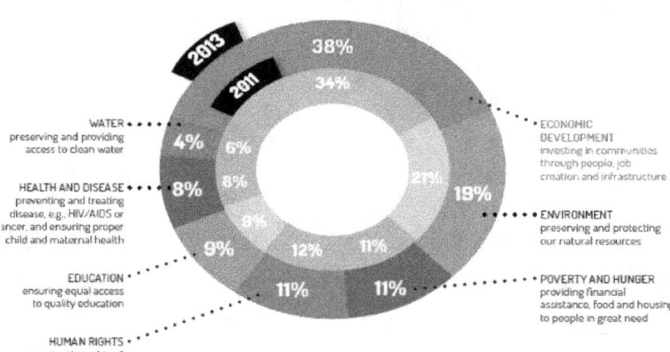

[13, pg.13]

Among those Fair Trade represents one of the most important dimension of ethical consumerism [69, pg.9]. It is also found that CSR activities in the product-related activities category seem to be the ones that the respondents most often recognize, while the activities of the philanthropy category are recognized the least.

So as a summary, although a growing number of consumers are getting more conscious and informed on ethical and social issues and question brand's social purpose, the popular trend is to base their purchasing decision on traditional criteria such as price, quality, and convenience. It is unquestionable that CSR initiatives have certain effect on consumers' buying behavior. However, consumers may favor one type of social issue versus the other, so it is equally important for organizations to select credible CSR activities that are more relevant to consumer's needs and expectations. Another key finding is, few consumers are aware of the social responsibility of companies. Companies have to communicate their CSR efforts more effectively. Building the awareness and communicating it broadly and repeatedly, is critical to increase consumer's confidence.

Can companies do well by doing good?

Part IV – Research Design & Analysis

Can companies do well by doing good?

Chapter 9 - Research Design

At the beginning of my research, I carried out a preliminary search on CSR and related concepts on sustainability, corporate citizenship, and corporate philanthropy. After narrowing down my research into sub-topics, I reviewed the relevant literature on measurement of social performance, correlation between social performance and corporate financial performance, consumer's response to CSR and leadership theories.

The mind mapping process of research design is illustrated below;

Figure 9.1 – Mind mapping process of research design

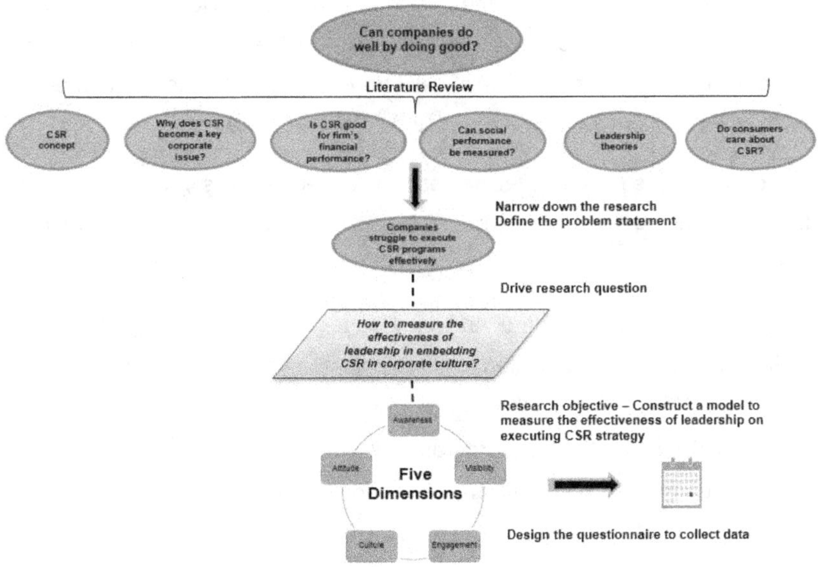

My findings from the literature review is, there is clearly a shift in corporate attitude to 'doing well and doing good' and many organizations have adopted the CSR codes of conduct and embedded CSR into business strategy. Yet, despite the growing emphasis on CSR, companies struggle to develop and implement CSR programs successfully. The biggest challenge with CSR is seen at the execution phase. The task is even more challenging for MNEs (multi-national enterprise).

Most of the CSR programs for larger organizations are initiated at corporate head-quarters. The task is typically managed by separate division in charge of coordinating the various aspects of CSR initiatives from development to communication and from execution to PR management. Most of the time, the vision is clouded, or the initiative loses it importance when it flows down the reporting chain. My further analysis on studying examples from successful CSR programs that impose positive impact on communities and environment, leads me to conclusion that leadership is one of the most critical elements for companies with strong CSR.

Understanding the positive outcomes that an effective CSR strategy could bring for an organization and the critical role of leadership, it brings the question that I address in this research - "How do we measure the effectiveness of leadership in embedding CSR in corporate culture?"

In order to measure the effectiveness of leadership, this research aims to develop a model, with the name 'CAAVE' by responding to the following questions;

- Are employees aware of and knowledgeable in CSR concepts?
- Are employees motivated to participate and support CSR activities?
- Is CSR visible within the organization?
- Is CSR integrated into corporate culture?
- Do employees have responsibility and accountability for CSR?

Each question leads to classification of a dimension as described below;

- Awareness – General knowledge and self-awareness on CSR concepts
- Attitude – Individual point of view on CSR and how they see CSR creating shared value for business and society
- Communication - Visibility of CSR within the organization and the effectiveness of communication channel
- Culture – Integration of CSR in corporate identity (HR system, performance review, job responsibility, etc.)
- Engagement – Level of responsibility and accountability on CSR strategy

In order to identify variables for each dimension, the five research questions are sub-divided into specific investigative questions, which become the building blocks of my questionnaire. Attributes variables (age, gender, division, and country) are collected optionally and not part of any rating. Each question is scored independently between 1 (low) to 5 (high) and the average score of all investigative questions rolls out as a decimal number for each dimension for each respondent. The average of all respondent's dimension scores sums up to be the rating for the overall company score. The following Kiviat diagram illustrates how the individual scores and the overall company score is plotted as an example. The data requirements table and point system for questionnaire is described in Appendix H and Appendix I.

Figure 9.2 – Design of 'CAAVE' model

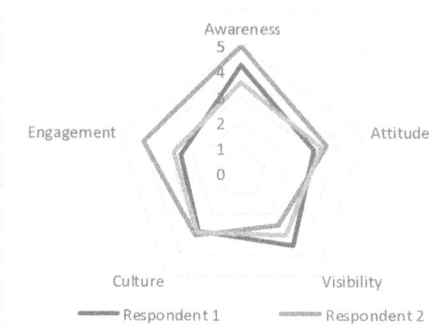

As a research method, I adopted both qualitative (interview) and quantitative (survey) methods. The primary data was collected by conducting a series of interviews with departmental leaders and an online survey with employees. The reason of adopting multiple methods (both qualitative and quantitative) is to avoid the bias. The target audience for interview was managers, where the survey was run for employees. By collecting data from two ends, I had a chance to cross-check my findings and harmonize the input to drive more insightful conclusions.

The table below summarizes the research questions and the corresponding interview and survey questions. The interview and survey questionnaires are listed at Appendix C and Appendix D.

Table– Matrix of Research Questions

Research Questions	Interview Questions	Survey Questions	Dimensions
Are employees aware of and knowledgeable in CSR concepts?	Q1-Q3	Q1-Q4	Awareness on CSR
Are employees motivated to participate and support CSR activities?	Q4-Q6	Q5-Q7	Personal Attitude/Motivation

Is CSR visible within the organization?	Q7-Q8	Q8-Q10	Visibility of CSR
Is CSR integrated into corporate culture?	Q9-Q11	Q11-Q14	Corporate Culture
Do employees have responsibility and accountability for CSR?	Q12-Q14	Q15-Q19	Employee Engagement

My research focused on multinational corporations with strong CSR reputation. Strong CSR reputation means that the company has a proven track record of CSR, publishes comprehensive corporate sustainability/responsibility reports, has good press release on CSR domain and has dedicated CSR team in place. Multinational corporations are companies that operate in one or more countries other than their home country. Based on this criteria, I selected IBM as my research company which has a global presence across more than 170 countries, ranked in top 30 in the Global CSR RepTrak and leading pioneering several initiatives in education, economic development, environmental sustainability and healthcare in CSR domain.

My design choice for the unit of analysis was individual. The participants for interviews were selected from a range of functional leaders from sales, marketing, operation, consulting and HR departments who have broader responsibility for all the functions within a specific geography or carrying specific responsibility for a broader region.

The majority of the interviews were conducted f2f. The interview was planned to take 30 min maximum to complete. There were no audio recordings to assure anonymity and encourage open discussion. The interview format was comprised of a set of structured questions. Probing questions were used carefully depending on the level of openness of the interviewee, and in most cases avoided.

I followed five-phased cycle as described by R. Kin (2011) in his book 'Qualitative Research from Start to Finish' [116, pg.178] to analyze and interpret my data on key questions 1,3 and 5 respectively. The analysis of the qualitative data was done manually. I used grounded theory framework to categorize my data by coding. I disassembled the data by selecting words, phrases from the responses and grouping them first at the basic and later in the higher conceptual level. In the third phase, I re-coded my data looking for patterns and associations across groups and finally reassembling them in a more abstract fashion to lead to broader conceptual themes.

I used self-selecting sampling technique to identify a list of individuals to take part in my search voluntarily. Then I used snowballing technique to further identify individuals in each country whereby the participants were asked to refer others who were interested in taking part in the research. The questions were a combination of list questions (multiple selection), category questions (one selection) and rating questions (scale 1 to 5). The last section in the survey had the respondent 's demographics such as age, gender and location.

The survey was rolled out as self-administered questionnaire where respondents could access the link digitally using their smart phones, tablets or simply using browsers on their desktops. The survey software was designed by a technology start-up providing basic analytics. Then I used Excel software to further analyze the data using the guide developed by J. Leahy [118].

Chapter 10 – Research Analysis

Figure 10.1 – Survey respondents

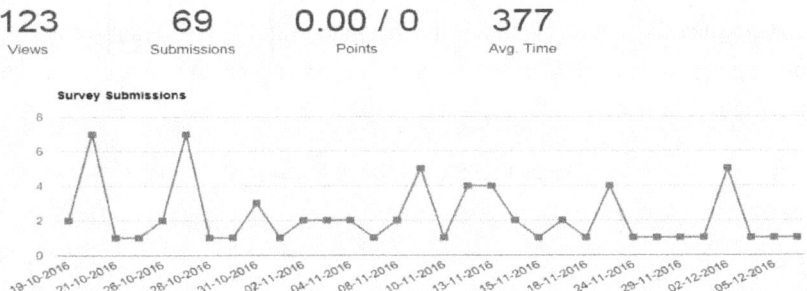

The survey invitation was distributed by email to 113 employees. Among those, 69 completed the survey leading to a response rate of 61%. The interview invitation is sent to 17 managers. 10 interviews were scheduled with a completion rate of 59%. Among those, 2 interviews were conducted over the phone. Considering the fact that the typical response rate is 35% [122, pg.222] in similar studies, the actual response rate being much higher, indicates that CRS is a topic of interest to many individuals.

Research participants were from 32 countries; 80% being located in Europe, 6% in North-America, and 14% in Middle-East and Africa. Male respondents correspond to 68% of the total respondents. 77% of participants is between 30-50 years old and 83% work in Sales & Marketing division.

The detailed findings from the research analysis is summarized in five sections, each corresponding to one of the dimensions.

Awareness on CSR

One out of every four respondents defined CSR as 'taking initiatives on environmental issues" and 'conducting business ethnically', and majority respondents indicated that the driving force behind CSR is 'environmental concerns' and 'brand reputation'. These findings are consistent with the literature review which suggests that CSR is moving into a more strategic dimension, and environmental challenges as mentioned in 'Global Risks Landscape' report and brand awareness as estimated by 'Reputation Institute' are the main drivers for companies to engage in CSR. The details of coding and categorization of interview data on this question can be found in Appendix E for Q1.

Figure 10.2 – Survey responses on CSR definition & drivers

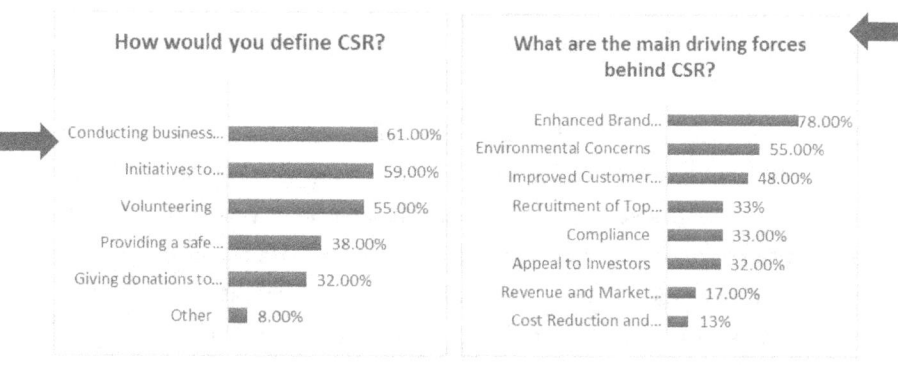

Although majority of the respondents confirmed the importance of CSR, their level of confidence and resourcefulness suggests that their understanding is limited to basic knowledge. As an example, when interviewees were asked to give examples of sustainable corporate actions that imposed positive impact, majority talked about general activities such as volunteering, helping charities, sponsoring community events, rather than giving specific examples. Very few gave examples from specific CSR initiatives.

Another observation from the interview sessions is respondents defined CSR in a broader scope using terms such as sustainability, corporate citizenship alternatively. This is the same approach taken in this paper where CSR is used as an umbrella concept for all corporate initiatives related to community development, environment concerns, etc.

According to survey participants, almost half of the population suggested that companies with strong CSR reputation have clear and actionable vision, and high employee engagement.

Figure 10.3 – Survey responses on successful CSR characteristics

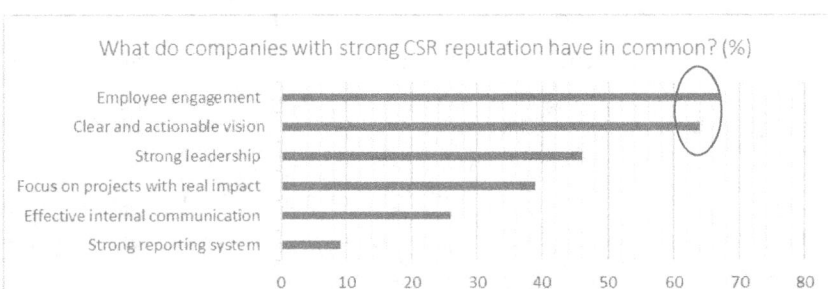

On the same question, interviewees pointed out that companies with strong CSR reputation are consistent with their strategy across all operating units regardless of the country of origin and legislative environment. They also have strong CSR governance in place; they know what they want to achieve, they select projects in a structured way, and in alignment with the needs of the community. They typically work in consumer-based industries with direct access to consumers and see CSR as their duty rather than positioning it to increase profitability.

The further analysis of the interview data leads to conclusion that project selection with real impacts and strong leadership is key for successful CSR implementation. There is a different point of view between interview (managers) and survey (employees) respondents, where managers position leadership as the primary influencer and see leadership responsible for many elements including strong governance, global execution and employee engagement. The details of coding and categorization of interview data can be found in Appendix E for Q3.

According to interviewees' point of view, authenticity is critical for companies to select the right projects that they can have more impact. Companies should choose projects that they can convey their unique experience to communities. As an example, IBM's success in CSR comes from using its technological expertise and know-how in specific areas such as education and healthcare to create a bigger impact for communities. This influence is to certain extend applicable for governments, where they do not possess the same level of practical know-how as corporates do and could benefit from this partnership. As quoted by one of the interviewees, companies should help communities to build the bakery, but should not be in the business of teaching them to sell breads.

As a summary, there is a strong evidence of awareness found on CSR among the employees (including survey and interview respondents). Almost all the respondents reported positively on their knowledge and interest to CSR, which is in line with literature review arguing that CSR is an area of growing importance for many stakeholders including employees. Majority confirmed that selection of projects that is connected to company's unique experience is critical for the success.

Attitude on CSR

The response to the key question on 'if business has a social responsibility beyond making a profit', introduced some debatable topics among interviewees. More than half of the participants claimed that business has a responsibility to give back to community, nurture the society and make the world a better place. Otherwise their presence would be exploitative, and this is against the basic principle of societal development. Opponents of this view claimed that the number one priority of business is to make profit to grow and as they grow, they create jobs. According to them providing employment should be treated as the biggest contribution to the community. They don't believe business can act without profitability in their mission unless it is a charity.

Others suggested that profit and social responsibility should not be mixed and putting profit in the agenda of CSR would destroy the purpose. Business should have a moral component, but profit expectation should not be mixed with the purpose of CSR. Expecting moral obligation to be the sole driver for business and expecting companies to trade off profit for goodwill would be a delusion. Yet, there should be a balance. The general consensus including the reflection from survey respondents (80% combined for rating 4 & 5) is that business has a social responsibility beyond making profit and should contribute to the well-being and development of the communities.

83% of survey respondents and the majority of interview participants confirmed that CSR would affect firm's value positively. Yet, they also mentioned that it is difficult to put a dollar value to CSR as some of the benefits would be intangible and hard to measure as the benefits are not realized immediately. Indeed, this is consistent with the findings in Chapter 4.

Another common commentary was the downside of having a negative CSR image is much bigger than the upside of having a positive image, which again is in-line with the outcome of the previous studies done in this field as highlighted in Chapter 2. According to view of some interviewees, not doing

CSR is not an option, but a key requirement for companies in order to conduct business. Companies cannot work in a market if they are not CSR compliant or have a bad image, which would have negative effect on their business results. Besides CSR could be a great door opener for companies if it is managed wisely. Some respondents commented that CSR even plays a more strategic role for global companies like IBM, as these initiatives broaden the knowledge and experience of their employees working in different cultures and bringing new business ideas.

Interviewees mostly touched the areas such as improved customer loyalty, increased employee motivation being the key areas that impact firm's value indirectly. The further analysis of the qualitative data leads to conclusion that CSR initiatives can enhance business value by retaining top talent in their workforce as employees are consciously drawn to work for ethnical companies, and secondly by improving customer loyalty as customers favor their decision for companies which demonstrate goodwill. The details of coding and categorization of interview data can be found in Appendix E for Q5. However, none of the interviewees mentioned anything about CSR's potential benefits of decreased operational costs, creating competitive advantage and appeal to investors, some of the business benefits noted in the literature review.

Another important observation from both survey and interview respondents is that half of the participants do not make their purchasing decisions often based on firm's or product's CSR reputation.

Figure 10.4 – Behavior on CSR as consumer during purchasing

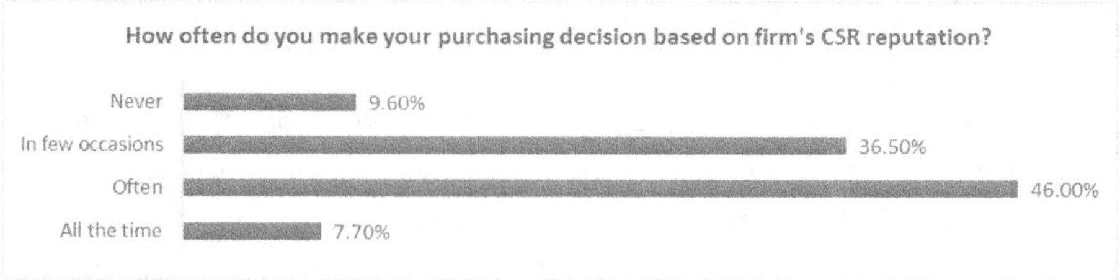

How often do you make your purchasing decision based on firm's CSR reputation?

Never	9.60%
In few occasions	36.50%
Often	46.00%
All the time	7.70%

This was aligned with the conclusion on the sub-topic with the title "*Do consumers care about CSR?*" in Appendix D. Although interviewees confirmed that as consumers, they are getting more sensitive with CSR and their expectations from business is getting more demanding, yet this trend is not fully reflected in the same scale when it comes to purchasing. The narrow focus is on fair-trade products and environmental goods, yet the majority of the interviewees are not willing to sacrifice the quality or ready to pay a premium in support to firm's products with higher CSR reputation. They also feel that they do not have access to enough information to make a decision. On the other token, majority of the interviewees confirmed that they stay away from a brand/product if the company has a bad CSR reputation.

As a summary, employees' willingness and personal motivation to support CSR is rated very high in the organization. All employees firmly confirmed that CSR can contributive positively to enhance the value of organization and business has a social responsibility to contribute to the well-being and development of the communities. Yet, this consciousness and willingness is not fully reflected in their purchasing decision. As a consumer, they have a tendency to abandon a bad reputable company or product more than they favor a reputable company or product on CSR.

Communication on CSR

Looking at the high response rates over four key initiatives (48% to 72%), it suggests that information on CSR is widely communicated and employees are aware of the ongoing CSR programs.

Figure 10.5 – Awareness on CSR initiatives

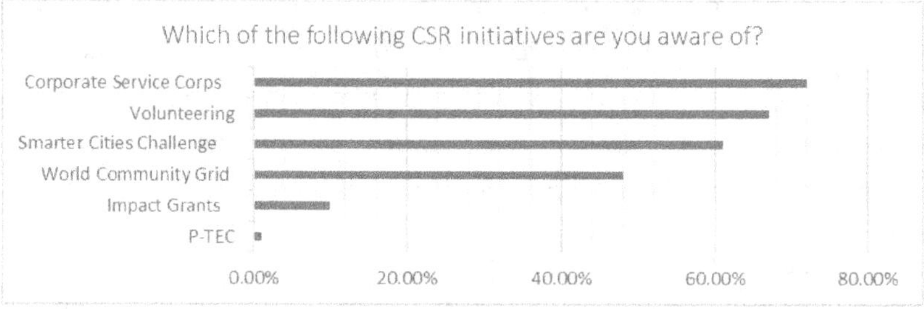

However, during the interview process, it is discovered that the two most selected initiatives; 'Volunteering' and 'Corporate Service Corps' are influenced by people, who have been participated in those programs earlier and promoted them within their community. So, the awareness is increased thru word of mouth communication, which may have an influence in the range of 6% to 11%.

52% of respondents said that they receive CSR-related communication once a quarter. 40% claim that they receive it more often. 6% deny receiving any information. Maybe, it is not frequent, but still there is some sort of CSR-related communication across the organization.

Figure 10.6 – Frequency of Communication

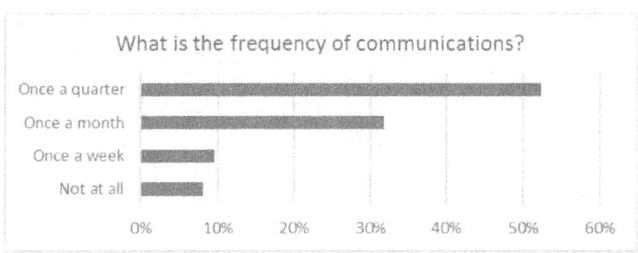

In addition, the findings from the method of communication is positive. A variety of channels are used to communicate CSR related information. Interview respondents indicated that time to time they browse corporate website and internal community to access further information and majority confirmed that they follow the information mostly thru social networking sites. It is found from survey responses that among all communication channels, social media (80%) is the most effective and the preferred one by employees.

Table – Communication Channel

Channel for Communication	# Selected	%
Social media	55	80
Website	49	71
Annual report	41	59
Emails	24	35
Meetings	21	30
Orientation Sessions	18	26
Training	12	17
Other	5	7

As a summary, maybe not frequent, but there is still an effective communication mechanism within the organization, utilizing a variety of different channels. Social media is proven to be the most effective and desired communication channel among employees.

Culture on CSR

The general feeling among employees on the importance given to CSR in the company is positive. Over 64% feels that CSR is important part of corporate culture. On a parallel question, over 53% of respondents believed that organization has increased its focus on CSR over the past couple of years.

Figure 10.7 – Importance given to CSR

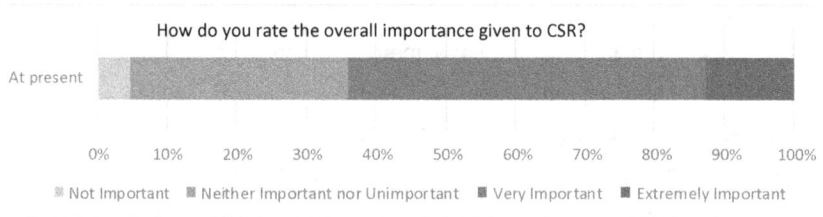

Although the overall importance given to CSR is rated positively and CSR programs are in general known and embraced by many, further questions on CSR's linkage to job responsibilities and performance reviews, proves that CSR strategy is detached from daily operation. Over 92% of respondents claimed that CSR is neither part of their job responsibilities nor performance reviews. From this outlook, it is clear that CSR strategy is initiated and managed centrally, with no specific KPIs or responsibilities pushed down to the reporting chain.

Figure 10.8 – Integration of CSR in corporate identity

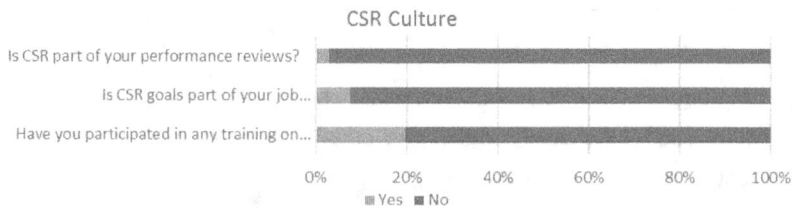

Considering the broader scope of CSR, it is understandable that employees didn't go through a formal training on CSR unless they work directly in communications department. Yet there are several digital and on-site trainings available and there are also some mandatory courses enforced by the company frequently on specific topics like integrity, supply-chain, diversity, etc. So, although the percentage of employees participating formal CSR training is less than 20%, this is not due to company's ignorance on the topic, but preference to a specific, and more focused delivery mechanism.

As a summary, although there is a positive feeling among employees about company's focus on CSR, there is a very weak evidence of CSR being connected to employee's daily responsibilities and KPIs. CSR strategy is not integrated into corporate culture.

Engagement on CSR

Considering the weak evidence of CSR culture observed within the organization, it is not surprising that only one-third of the employees (36%) are engaged in CSR activities. Among them, the majority responded that they are engaged in CSR as they believe it is the right thing to do. Only 4% said that they are engaged because it is required from them. Another important finding of the research is, one third of the respondents said that they'd like to participate if the right opportunity is given. This proves the point again that employees are getting more conscious and interested in CSR, yet they struggle to maximize their contribution if the right conditions are not set up for them.

Figure 10.9 – Reason of participation into CSR activities

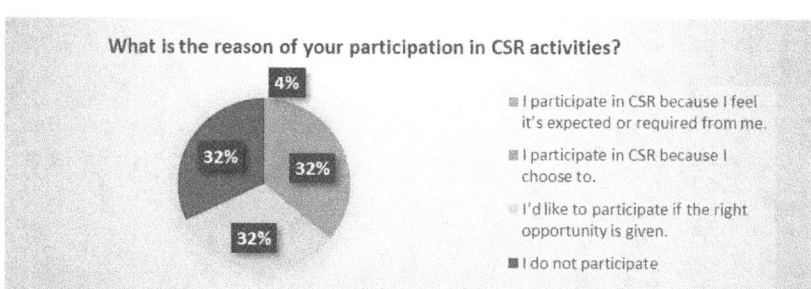

Analyzing the responses, it seems that employees feel no pressure or motivation from the up-line managers to engage in CSR as part of their job responsibility. Couple of interviewees discussed about a few incentives and rewards programs in place, yet those programs are either not promoted properly or not effective, as the awareness is very limited. Looking at the common characteristics of high performing CSR organizations as discussed in Chapter 2, the company fails to demonstrate such characteristics to foster a culture of CSR. So, the influence of leadership team and the HR system in place to encourage employees for their active participation into CSR program is almost negligible.

'Volunteering' and 'Donations' are the most participated activities. Employees spend majority of their CSR activities in support to community in the areas of kid's education and other social causes.

Figure 10.10 – Type of CSR activities

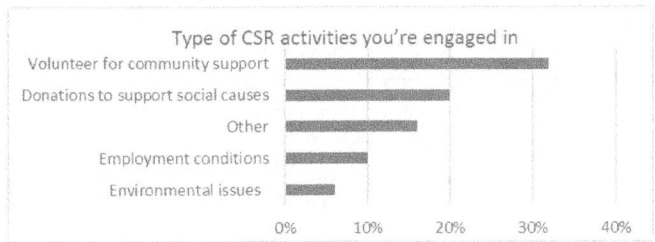

As a summary, the employee engagement level in CSR programs is reported very low in the organization. Even observing the active participants, their motivation is mostly due to self-interest rather than corporate direction. There is very little evidence of programs for rewarding and incentivizing CSR decisions and initiatives that would trigger more motivations for active engagement.

Research Analysis Summary

Based on the CAAVE model developed during this study, <u>the overall company score</u> is illustrated in the Kiviat diagram below. The rating of attitude is relatively high in comparison to other dimensions, where the culture and engagement scored poorly.

Figure 10.11 – Overall Company score *(1 Low 5 High)*

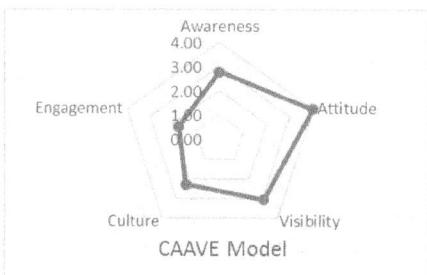

Dimension	Score
Awareness	2.79
Attitude	4.00
Visibility	3.05
Culture	2.29
Engagement	1.73

The **main findings of the research** are summarized below;

- There is a strong and positive view on how employees see CSR creating shared value both for the business and the society
- There is a medium-high level of awareness on CSR at individual level
- Social media is seen as the most effective and preferred communication channel for CSR related matters
- CSR strategy is disconnected from the daily operation; it is neither part of employees' job responsibilities nor performance reviews
- The level of employee engagement in CSR is very low

The <u>secondary findings of the research</u> are summarized below;

- Although employees respond positively about CSR, when it comes to making a decision as consumers, most of the time their buying behavior is not consistent
- The downside of having a negative CSR image is much bigger than the upside of having a positive image

- Consumers do not seek for CSR reputation by default, but have a tendency to stay away from bad reputable companies
- Environmental challenges and brand awareness are the main drivers for companies to engage in CSR
- Selection of projects with high impact and having a strong leadership in place are the key elements for successful implementation of CSR

Limitations

The findings of this study must be viewed in the context of several limitations. The focus on a large multi-national company limits the generalizability of the findings. The size and the territorial coverage of a company plays a critical role in company's level of commitment to CSR. Typically, large organizations create CSR departments to coordinate the CSR initiatives, where in small businesses, the owner is mostly likely the sole decision maker on CSR programs. As a result, the research for small and medium size enterprises operating locally or privately-owned companies may lead to different findings.

Another limitation is the selection of the organizational type, which is business-to-business. Choosing a business-to-consumer organizational type may lead to different findings, as CSR is known to be more effective in consumer-oriented industries.

In this study a US firm is selected. To enhance the validity of findings, I recommend similar research to be done for companies with their headquarters located in countries with different cultural background and/or at different economic development stage.

This study has also limitations due to time constraints. The interview process was completed in 4 weeks and the administration of the survey was taken over 8-weeks period. So, the data collection is a snapshot of the company at a particular time-frame. Employee's view on CSR may change over time and as well their engagement with the changes in their job responsibilities. A longitudinal research run over 3 or 4 quarters, would support the collection of more unbiased data.

The research was not able to reach min sample size; 384 for surveys and 15-20 interviews as suggested by M. Saunders, P. Lewis, A. Thornhill [122, pg.219, 235]. This is partially related to time constraints. Running the search for a longer period, would increase the sample size to the required number.

80% data is collected from Europe and there is no representation from Asia Pacific and Latin America regions, which accounts for 2/3rd of the entire workforce for IBM. 83% of participants are also from 'Sales & Marketing' department. The increase of sampling from different countries and divisions may ensure that the findings are more reliable and representative to the whole organization.

As the interviews are conducted using single-informant technique, all respondents being from one firm, and all data is collected with a common method, the general conclusions drawn are based on the information gathered from the respondents. There might be an issue of bias where the responses might not fully be captured by researcher (myself) and may reflect the views of the researcher instead of the participants'. Also like in many interviews, there may be an issue of response bias, where respondents may have a tendency to make themselves more CSR oriented and friendly than they normally are. The extension of the analysis is recommended for smaller and local companies and additional research should employ multi-informant and multimethod designs to overcome this potential limitation.

Can companies do well by doing good?

Part V - Conclusion

Can companies do well by doing good?

Conclusions

Over the last decade, CSR has become a mainstream activity and majority of the organizations have adopted CSR codes of conduct as part of their corporate strategy. Customers, governments, consumers and investors continue to pressure companies to act more sustainably and responsibly for present and for the future. As a result of this, companies incorporated environmental and social strategies into their operations and they were committed to doing things more than legally required. **CSR is no longer a philanthropic or an authentic thing to do, but a strategic initiative** being part of corporate strategy for many organizations.

CSR doesn't happen spontaneously; **it is a complex and strategic endeavor** that demands considerable attention and commitment from the organization. It has to be designed carefully with long-term vision, in alignment with HR systems, and with right engagement model to maximize the impact.

Managing and executing CSR is even a more challenging task for multi-national enterprises. The findings of the study reveal the fact that even if the company has dedicated resources and goodwill, **embedding CSR into the DNA of an organization is not a trivial task**. We have seen from the research results that even if the awareness at the individual level remains high, and employees in general have a strong view on how CSR creates shared value both for the business and the society, if the vision on CSR is not clearly and persistently communicated within the organization, if the right environment is not setup to encourage active participation, and if CSR strategy is not linked to daily operations, then CSR programs run into a risk of being under-utilized, weakened, and ultimately turning into local PR projects.

Leaders play a critical role in integrating business and social needs and successfully executing CSR programs. It is leader's responsibility to set up an actionable direction and drive active engagement within the organization. Looking at the examples of successful CSR initiatives and analyzing leaders who inspired others with their approach, we observe that CSR requires responsible, charismatic, iconoclastic leaders who are progressive, trustworthy, compassionate and courageous, leaders who can challenge status-quo and embrace counterintuitive ideas, leaders who can think in the long-term and integrate sustainability into core business strategy with consistent behavior. Yet, even if companies have charismatic and visionary leaders in place, there remains a challenge on how to measure the influence of leadership in embedding CSR into corporate culture in a structured way.

The **CAAVE model** developed in this study provides a foundation to close this gap and help companies assess the effectiveness of CSR in five dimensions; culture, awareness, attitude, visibility and engagement. So, adopting this model, companies can measure their internal readiness for CSR, benchmark their progress over time, and eventually measure the effectiveness of leadership. The CAAVE model applied for the selected multi-national enterprise in this study, highlighted some areas for improvements from effective communication to tighter integration of CSR strategy to daily operations, from active employee engagement to better design of HR systems, which might be difficult to explore and document otherwise. The model is yet to be revised to incorporate characteristics of different industries, business types (B2B, B2C), organization types (multi-national, local, large, small) and country of origin.

Despite the fact that there is a positive momentum and transparency towards CSR, CSR spending represents still a small portion of the corporate revenue. According to CECP (Committee Encouraging Corporate Profit), the median total giving for American companies was 0.13% of their revenue [10, pg.40]. It is not in the scope of this book to do a trend analysis to measure the companies' spending on CSR. On the other token, it will be useful to conduct a further study to analyze if the positive trend seen in CSR is also reflected in corporate investments in terms of ratio to revenue and whether this would be a good metric to evaluate company's performance.

It is also important to highlight the fact that the business values are in constant transformation. Currently business goals are re-evaluated, more in-line with welfare, fairness and justice. A great example of this transformation is Benefit Corporations, which redefine the boundaries of business. These new type of business entities are not required to maximize profits and can decide to reinvest in community and the environment without the risks of being opposed or slowed down by shareholders. There are already thirty states in US that allow the formation of benefit corporations. [86]

Another key development is the foundation of entities like B Team. In 2013, R. Branson and J. Zeitz launched a global initiative by a group of business leaders to drive transformational change in the business and to ensure business becomes a driving force for social, environmental and economic benefit. B Team sets a mission to catalyze a better way of doing business and prioritize people and planet alongside profit and help business focus away from short term gain and to balance the long-term benefits for people and planet. [87]

Path forward from here is, CSR will continue to evolve to become more tactical, more collaborative and more integrated. Visser (2013) call this new era "**Age of Responsibility**", where a new model of CSR focuses on understanding the interconnections in the macro level system (societies, communities, economies and ecosystems) and changing a company's strategy to optimize the outcomes for larger human and ecological system [94, pg.6]. With the rise of mission-driven non-profit organizations, emergence of new business leaders, development of next generation business entities, influence of younger generations joining the workforce, responsible governments, and more savvy and conscious consumers, CSR initiatives will move beyond philanthropic, marginal, image-driven projects to more strategic and cause-driven partnerships, where corporate resources would be maximized to address critical social and environmental challenges and drive social innovation and transformation in various areas.

Appendices

Can companies do well by doing good?

Appendix A – Instruments of CSR

The existing frameworks distinguish from each other being normative, management and reporting frameworks. UN Global Compact principles and OECD Guidelines provide normative frameworks where ISO 26000 is more a management standard and GRI is a reporting standard. [44, pg.25] The details are enclosed.

- **ISO 26000** is one of the recognized international standard for CSR. It helps clarify what social responsibility is and helps businesses and organizations translate principles into effective actions. It is aimed at all types of organizations regardless of activity, size or location [44, pg.26]. Its goal is to contribute to global sustainable development by encouraging business to practice social responsibility to improve their impacts on their workers, their natural environments and their communities. It addresses seven core subjects of social responsibility as illustrated below.

-

Figure A.1 – Social Responsibility: 7 Core Subjects

[16, pg.9]

- **Global Reporting Initiative (GRI)** provides sustainability reporting guidelines in measuring and reporting economic, environmental, social and governance performance indicators. Currently, almost 1400 companies worldwide are following the GRI guidelines (GRI 2002, 2010). In 2010 about 1.500 companies published CSR or sustainability reports based on the GRI guidelines [pg.17]. GRI's guidelines align with international normative frameworks (OECD & UN as described below), allowing them to benefit from each initiatives' complementarities and strengths [44, pg.25].

- **OECD Guidelines for Multinational Enterprises** provides recommendations for responsible business conduct in areas such as employment and industrial relations, human rights, environment, information disclosure, combating bribery, consumer interests, science and technology, competition, and taxation.

- **UN Global Compact principles** is a set of 10 principles on human rights, labor standards, environmental standards, and anti-corruption measures, implemented by companies around the world on a voluntary basis. By now about 8,000 businesses and non-business stakeholders from 135 countries participate in this UN driven initiative [pg.16].

In addition to mentioned frameworks above, there are a number of rating indices developed that provide a method for comparing companies in the sustainable context. The most popular ones are the following;

- **Dow Jones Sustainability World Index (DJSI)** is the first global sustainability index launched in 1999. DJSI tracks the performance of the world's leading companies in terms of economic, environmental and social criteria and recognized by investors as the leading benchmarks for corporate sustainability [33]. S&P Dow Jones Indices partners with RobecoSAM, to provide investors with objective benchmarks for managing their sustainability investment portfolios.

- **FTSE4Good Index** is designed to measure the performance of companies demonstrating strong environmental, social and governance (ESG) practices. Transparent management and clearly-defined ESG criteria make FTSE4Good indices suitable tools to be used by a wide variety of market participants when creating or assessing responsible investment products. FTSE ESG ratings are designed to measure the ESG risk and performance of companies worldwide and provide market participants with a tool to be used in portfolio design and management against ESG criteria, or as a framework for corporate engagement and stewardship. [121]

- **Best Corporate Citizens**, conducted by the Corporate Responsibility Magazine, is known as one of the world's top corporate responsibility ranking. The data is based on publicly available information and each company is ranked in seven categories; environment, climate change, employee relations, human rights, corporate governance, financial performance and philanthropy & community support [25].

- **CSR RepTrak 100** is an annual study conducted by **Reputation Institute**, the world's leading reputation-based research advisory firm, to measure the reputation of companies in the United States through three dimensions; citizenship on how company supports good causes and protects environment, governance on how company behaves ethnically, and workplace on how company treats its employees [24].

- **Corporate Knights**, a Canadian based media and research company, produces corporate rankings based on corporate sustainability performance. Its best-known rankings include the Best 50 Corporate Citizens in Canada and the Global 100 Most Sustainable Corporations [34].

Last but not least, there are some tools offered as a service fee or subscription basis that could be leveraged to get some insight into company's sustainability efforts and rate them in comparison with other companies. Couple of them are listed below;

- **CSRHub** - World's largest sustainability business intelligence database with its ratings help benchmark, evaluate, and improve company sustainability performance. https://www.csrhub.com/

- **MultiCapital Scorecard** - An advanced 'Triple Bottom Line' measurement, management and reporting system to help companies understand if their operations are socially, environmentally and economically sustainable. http://www.multicapitalscorecard.com/

- **Global Initiative for Sustainability Ratings (GISR) CORE program** – Decision-making platform for all ESG stakeholders. For investors, it offers tools to select the most suitable ESG ratings products to optimize decision-making. For companies, it provides a framework to evaluate and benchmark their sustainability progress. http://ratesustainability.org/

Appendix B - Reference Organizations

(in alphabetic order)

B Lab is a non-profit organization that serves a global movement of people using business as a force for good. B Lab issues a private certification known as B Corp certification. To be granted and to preserve certification, companies must receive a minimum score on an online assessment for "social and environmental performance", satisfy the requirement that the company integrate B Lab commitments to stakeholders into company governing documents. https://www.bcorporation.net/what-are-b-corps/about-b-lab

Caux Round Table is an international network of principled business leaders working to promote a moral capitalism. The CRT advocates implementation of the CRT Principles for Business through which principled capitalism can flourish and sustainable and socially responsible prosperity can become the foundation for a fair, free and transparent global society. http://www.cauxroundtable.org/

CDP (Carbon Disclosure Project) is an organization based in the United Kingdom which works with shareholders and corporations to disclose the greenhouse gas emissions of major corporations. https://www.cdp.net/en-US/Pages/About-Us.aspx

CECP (The CEO Force for Good) is a coalition of CEOs united in the belief that societal improvement is an essential measure of business performance. Founded in 1999, CECP has grown to a movement of more than 150 CEOs of the world's largest companies across all industries. http://cecp.co/

Corporate Register, similar to GRI is another reporting initiatives around the world which provides its members access to global online directory of corporate responsibility reports. http://www.corporateregister.com/

European Sustainable Development Network (ESDN) is an informal network of public administrators and other experts who deal with sustainable development strategies and policies. The network covers all 27 EU Member States, plus other European countries. The ESDN is active in promoting sustainable development and facilitating the exchange of good practices in Europe and gives advice to policy-makers at the European and national levels. http://www.sd-network.eu/

Fair Labour Association (FLA) is a collaborative effort of universities, civil society organizations and socially responsible companies dedicated to protecting workers' rights around the world. FLA believes that all goods should be produced fairly and ethically and has a mission to improve workers' lives by encouraging companies implementing FLA's Code of Conduct across their supply chains, conducting external assessments and supporting compliance [26]. As an example, Apple is the first high-tech company in the industry joining the FLA, which is responsible for investigating Apple's suppliers and reporting the results to the public after Apple facing increased criticism and public pressure when it is discovered that half of Apple's suppliers have their workers work over 60 hours a week in their factories and 35% of suppliers fail to meet the safety standards [23, pg.24]. http://www.fairlabor.org/

Fairtrade is an alternative approach to conventional trade based on a partnership between producers and traders. Fairtrade serves small-scale farmers and workers in the least developed and developing countries. The international Fairtrade system - made up of Fairtrade International and its member organizations - represents the world's largest and most recognized fair-trade system. When a product carries the **FAIRTRADE Mark** it means the producers and traders have met Fairtrade Standards http://www.fairtrade.net/about-fairtrade.html

Global FoodBanking Network (GFN) is an international non-profit organization that fights world hunger by creating, supporting and strengthening food banks in communities where they are needed around the world and by supporting food banks where they exist. GFN currently supports food bank operations in 24 countries - representing more than one-third of the world's hungry. https://www.foodbanking.org/

Institute for Market ecology is an international body for the inspection, certification and quality control of organic, eco-friendly and socially-responsible products.

http://www.imo.ch/logicio/pmws/indexDOM.php?client_id=imo&page_id=home&lang_iso639=en

Justmeans is an online community and publisher of news about corporate social responsibility, sustainability, energy, health, education, technology and innovation for business professionals, executives, journalists, bloggers, academics and news organizations who are engaged with and interested in CSR. http://www.justmeans.com/

MSCI is an independent provider of research-driven insights and tools for institutional investors. MSCI ESG Research provides in-depth research, ratings and analysis of the environmental, social and governance-related business practices of thousands of companies worldwide. The research is designed to provide critical insights that can help institutional investors identify risks and opportunities that traditional investment research may overlook. https://www.msci.com/esg-integration

Organization for Economic Co-operation and Development (OECD) has a mission to promote policies that will improve the economic and social well-being of people around the world. OECD provides a forum in which governments can work together to share experiences and understand what drives economic, social and environmental change. http://www.oecd.org

Principle for Responsible Investment (PRI) is the world's leading proponent of responsible investment. Its goals are to understand the investment implications of environmental, social and governance issues and to support signatories in integrating these issues into investment and ownership decisions. The six Principles were developed by investors and are supported by the UN. https://www.unpri.org/about

Rainforest Alliance is an international non-profit organization that works to conserve biodiversity and ensure sustainable livelihoods. The Rainforest Alliance Certified™ seal is an internationally recognized symbol of environmental, social and economic sustainability that helps both businesses and consumers do their part to ensure a brighter future for us all. The certified farms and forests are managed according to rigorous environmental, social and economic criteria designed to conserve wildlife; safeguard soils and waterways; protect workers, their families and local communities; and increase livelihoods. http://www.rainforest-alliance.org/

Reputation Institute is the world's leading research and advisory firm for reputation. Reputation Institute's RepTrak® model is the gold standard for reputation measurement, providing a one-of-a-kind appraisal of how the general public views the world's best-known companies. https://www.reputationinstitute.com

SAI is a non-governmental, international, multi-stakeholder organization dedicated to improving workplaces and communities by developing and implementing socially responsible standards. In 1997, SAI launched **SA8000 (Social Accountability 8000)** – a voluntary standard for workplaces, which is currently used by businesses and governments around the world and is recognized as one of the strongest workplace standards. http://sa-intl.org/

United Nations Environment Program (UNEP) is the leading global environmental authority that sets the global environmental agenda, promotes the coherent implementation of the environmental dimension of sustainable development within the United Nations system and serves as an authoritative advocate for the global environment. http://www.unep.org/

United States Green Building Council (USGBC) is established in 1993 with a mission to promote sustainability-focused practices in the construction industry. USGBC developed a rating system, **Leadership in Energy and Environmental Design (LEED)** to evaluate the environmental performance of a building and encourage market transformation towards sustainable design. http://www.usgbc.org/leed

Established in 1971, **World Economic Forum** is a not-for-profit foundation, acting as a bridge-builder between the public sector, business and civil society to help political, business and other leaders of society to improve the state of the world.

http://www3.weforum.org

Can companies do well by doing good?

Appendix C – Interview Questions

Awareness

Q1) How would you define CSR?

Q2) Give examples of companies that imposed positive impact on communities and environment thru their sustainable corporate actions.

Q3) According to your view, what do companies with strong CSR reputation have in common?

Attitude

Q4) What do you think about this statement – "Business has a social responsibility beyond making a profit" and why?

Q5) Do you believe CSR activities can positively affect firm's value and how?

Q6) As a consumer/customer, when was the last time you choose a product/service based on firm's CSR reputation?

Communication

Q7) How often CSR-related information is communicated internally and thru what channel?

Q8) When was the last time you read something on your corporate CSR policy?

Culture

Q9) How do you rate the overall importance given to CSR within your organization?

Q10) How CSR is connected/integrated to your personal goals/responsibilities?

Q11) Have you participated/conducted any training on CSR?

Engagement

Q12) As a leader, how do you keep your employees updated with CSR policy matters?

Q13) How often do you reward/incentivize your team for their CRS initiatives and decisions?

Q14) Name couple of CRS initiatives that you've involved in or plan to involve in the previous/coming years.

Appendix D – Survey Questions

Awareness

This section is intended to assess general knowledge and self-awareness of respondents on CSR concepts.

Q1) How would you define Corporate Social Responsibility?

☐ Giving donations to charity   ☐ Volunteering

☐ Providing a safe working environment for employees   ☐ Do not know

☐ Taking initiatives to reduce the company's impact on the environment   ☐ Other (please specify)

☐ Conducting business in an ethical and professional manner

Q2) What are the main driving forces behind CSR?

☐ Enhanced Brand Reputation   ☐ Cost reduction and efficiency

☐ Appeal to investors   ☐ Environmental concern

☐ Recruitment of top talent   ☐ Compliance

☐ Improved customer loyalty   ☐ Revenue and market share

Q3) What do companies with strong CSR reputation have in common?

☐ Clear and actionable vision ☐ Strong leadership

☐ Focus on projects with real impact ☐ Employee engagement

☐ Effective internal communication ☐ Strong reporting system

Q4) What are the barriers preventing companies from carrying out CSR initiatives?

☐ Lack of funds/resources ☐ Cost/ Low Return on Investment

☐ Lack of knowledge ☐ Lack of staff awareness and willingness to participate in CSR activities

☐ Not appreciated by senior management ☐ Other

Attitude

This section is intended to explore the personal motivation of respondents on CSR concepts.

Q5) To what extend do you agree or disagree with the following statement – "Business has a social responsibility beyond making a profit"?

5-Highest and 1- Lowest

Q6) To what extent do you believe that CSR would enhance company reputation?

5-Highest and 1- Lowest

Q7) As a consumer, how often do you make your purchase decision based on firm's CSR reputation?

○ All the time

○ Often

○ In few occasions

○ Never

Communication

This section is intended to measure the visibility of CSR within the organization and the effectiveness of internal communication.

Q8) Which channels are used to communicate CSR policy matters?

☐ Orientation sessions   ☐ Social media

☐ Training   ☐ Meetings

☐ Newsletter   ☐ Annual report

☐ Emails   ☐ Website

Q9) What is the frequency of communications?

○ Once a quarter

○ Once a month

○ Once a week

○ Not at all

Q10) Which of the following corporate-wide CSR initiatives are you aware of?

☐ Corporate Service Corps   ☐ Volunteering

☐ Smarter Cities Challenge   ☐ World Community Grid

☐ Impact Grants   ☐ P-TEC

Culture

This section is intended to evaluate how CSR is integrated in corporate identity.

Q11) How do you rate the overall importance given to CSR within IBM?

○ Not Important

○ Neither Important nor Unimportant

○ Very Important

○ Extremely Important

Q12) Have you participated in any training on CSR/sustainability?

○ Yes ○ No

Q13) Is CSR goals part of your job description/responsibility?

○ Yes ○ No

Q14) Is CSR part of your performance reviews?

○ Yes ○ No

Q15) Do you believe that IBM has increased its focus on CSR over the past two years?

○ Not at all   ○ A little

○ A lot   ○ Not sure

Engagement

This section is intended to assess if respondents have CSR responsibilities (and accountability) and their level of engagement with ongoing CSR programs.

Q16) Are you engaged in any formal CSR activities as part of your job responsibility?

○ Yes

○ No

Q17) What is the reason of your participation in CSR activities?

☐ I participate in CSR because I feel it is expected or required from me.

☐ I'd like to participate if the right opportunity is given.

☐ I participate in CSR because I choose to.

☐ I do not participate.

Q18) Type of CSR activities you're engaged in?

☐ Volunteer for community support

☐ Donations to support social causes

☐ Environmental issues

☐ Employment conditions

☐ Other

Q19) Do you get reward/incentives for your contribution in CRS initiatives?

○ Yes

○ No

Background Information

This section consists of general questions.

Q20) Your gender

Male, Female

Q21) Your age

20-30, 31-40, 40-50, +50

Q22) In which country are you located in?

Q23) Your division?

○ HR

◉ Sales & Marketing

○ Operations & Research

○ Consulting & Services

Legal, Finance

Q24) Number of employees reporting to you?

○ Less than 10   ○ Between 10 and 50

○ Between 50 and 250   ○ Over 250

Can companies do well by doing good?

Appendix E - Coding and Analysis of Interview Data

Question 1 - How would you define CSR?	
Open Coding	
Giving back to community	Support expertise and infrastructure for education
Volunteering activities	
Commitment for better community	Help society move forward
Treating their workforce	Social entrepreneurship
Goodwill of corporates	Make positive contributions to community
Providing support to help country grow	Develop future leaders
Interaction with society ethnically	Engagement with local communities
Act on environmental issues	Influence and change the system regardless of legislative environment
Axial Coding	
Volunteering	Support education
Environmental issues	Support startup communities
Support community well-being	Support social causes
Selective Coding	
Socially Responsible Business Practices (support social causes, develop leaders)	
Employee engagement (volunteering)	
Corporate Philanthropy (support education, support startup communities)	
Corporate Social Marketing (support community, environment)	

Question 3 - What do companies with strong CSR reputation have in common?	
Open Coding	
Depends on employee's motivation	DNA of the company
Strong vision	Mature leadership
Focusing on the field that can make more impact	Global, strong brand
Authenticity	Companies with consumer product line
Strong corporate culture	CSR governance
Access the resources	Consistent globally
Multi-national companies	Enlightened leadership
Project oriented	Projects alignment with need
See CSR as duty	Strong leadership
Axial Coding	
Employee motivation	Multi-national companies
Vision	Leadership
Project oriented	Consumer-focused companies
Strong CSR culture	
Selective Coding	
Employee engagement (employee motivation)	
Leadership	
Projects with real impact (project-oriented, multi-national companies, consumer-focused companies)	
Vision (vision, strong CSR culture)	

Question 5 – Do you believe CSR activities can positively affect firm's value and how?	
Open Coding	
Millenniums will work for responsible companies	Increase profitability
Goodwill of the company	Consumers feel empathy to brand products
Employees broaden their perspective	Build loyalty
Bring new opportunities to business	Ensure making business when compliant
Increase the market share	Employees tend to work for ethnical companies
	Impact brand image
Axial Coding	
Employee recruitment	Higher employee engagement
Brand image	Increased revenue
	Employee retention
Selective Coding	
Recruitment and retention of top talent (employee recruitment, employee retention, higher employee engagement)	
Improved customer loyalty (brand image)	
Increased revenue	

Can companies do well by doing good?

Appendix F - Data Requirements Table

Investigative Questions	Variables required	Detail in which data measured
Q1	Opinion of respondent on CSR	Giving donations to charity, volunteering, providing a safe working environment, Reduce the company's impact on the environment, conducting business ethically
Q2	Opinion of respondent on driving forces behind CSR	Brand Reputation, cost reduction and efficiency, appeal to investors, environmental concern, recruitment of top talent, compliance, customer loyalty, revenue
Q3	Opinion of respondent on strong CSR characteristics	Clear vision, strong leadership, projects with real impact, employee engagement, communication, reporting system
Q4	Opinion of respondent on inhibitors of CSR	Lack of resources, lack of knowledge/awareness, lack of management support, cost
Q5	Opinion of respondent if business has a social responsibility	1 Lowest 5 Highest
Q6	Opinion of respondent on if CSR adds value to business	1 Lowest 5 Highest
Q7	Behavior of respondent as a consumer on CSR	All the time, often, in few occasions, never
Q8	Opinion of respondent on communication channel	Orientation sessions, social media, training, meetings, newsletter, annual report, emails, website
Q9	Opinion of respondent on communication frequency	Once a week/month/quarter, never
Q10	Opinion of respondent on CSR initiatives	Service Corps, volunteering, smarter cities, community grid, impact Grants, P-TEC
Q11	Opinion of respondent on importance of CSR	Not important, very important, extremely important
Q12	Behavior of respondent on CSR training	Yes No
Q13	Behavior of respondent on CSR	Yes No

		job responsibility	
Q14	Behavior of respondent on CSR performance reviews	Yes No	
Q15	Opinion of respondent on company's focus on CSR	A lot, a little, not sure, not at all	
Q16	Behavior of respondent on CSR engagement	Yes No	
Q17	Behavior of respondent on CSR participation	Participate because it is expected, participate if there is opportunity, participate because of own will, do not participate	
Q18	Behavior of respondent on CSR activities	Volunteer, environmental, donations, employment conditions	
Q19	Behavior of respondent on CSR incentives	Yes No	
Q20-24	Attribute of respondent on gender, age, country, division, # of employees in reporting chain	Various	

Appendix H – Point System for Questionnaire

Dimensions	Questions	1	2	3	4	5
Awareness	Q1	Do not know	Min 2 selection other than 'Do not Know'	Min 3 selection other than 'Do not Know'	Min 4 selection other than 'Do not Know'	All 5 selection other than 'Do not Know'
	Q2	Less than 2 selections	2 selections	Min 3 selections	Min 4 selections	+5 selections
	Q3	Less than 2 selections	2 selections	3 selections	4 selections	+5 selections
	Q4	Less than 2 selections	2 selections	3 selections	4 selections	+5 selections
Attitude	Q5	1	2	3	4	5
	Q6	1	2	3	4	5
	Q7	Never	-	In few occasions	Often	All the time
Visibility	Q8	Less than 3 selections	2 selections	3 selections	4 selections	+5 selections
	Q9	Not at all	-	Once a quarter	Once a month	Once a week
	Q10	Less than 2 selections	2 selections	3 selections	4 selections	+5 selections
Culture	Q11	Not important	-	Neither important or unimportant	Very important	Extremely important
	Q12-Q14	3 No	-	1 Yes 2 No	2 Yes 1 No	3 Yes
	Q15	Not at all	-	Not sure	A little	A lot
Engagement	Q16 & Q19	2 N	-	1 Yes 1 No	-	2 Yes
	Q17	I do not participate	-	I'd like to participate	I participate because I choose to	I participate because it is expected
	Q18	No selection	1 selection	2 selections	3 selections	+4 selections

139

Calculating Company Score		
Dimension	Question	Weight
Awareness		
	Q1	0.25
	Q2	0.25
	Q3	0.25
	Q4	0.25
Attitude		
	Q5	0.35
	Q6	0.3
	Q7	0.35
Visibility		
	Q8	0.3
	Q9	0.3
	Q10	0.4
Culture		
	Q11	0.2
	Q12-Q14	0.6
	Q15	0.2
Engagement		
	Q16 & Q19	0.5
	Q17	0.25
	Q18	0.25

Appendix J – List of Figures

References

[1] Forbes, 2013. *When It Comes to CSR, Size Matters.*
http://www.forbes.com/sites/insead/2013/08/14/when-it-comes-to-csr-size-matters/#52a7b40e1b6f

[2] KPMG, 2013. *Survey of Corporate Responsibility Reporting.*
https://www.kpmg.com/Global/en/IssuesAndInsights/ArticlesPublications/corporate-responsibility/Documents/kpmg-survey-of-corporate-responsibility-reporting-2013.pdf

[3] European Sustainable Development Network Quarterly Report, 2011. *Focus CSR: The New Communication of the EU Commission on CSR and National CSR Strategies and Action Plans.* http://www.sd-network.eu/quarterly%20reports/report%20files/pdf/2011-December-The_New_Communication_of_the_EU_Commission_on_CSR_and_National_CSR_strategies.pdf

[4] D. Trencansky, D. Tsaparlidis, 2014. *The effects of company´s age, size and type of industry on the level of CSR.* http://www.diva-portal.se/smash/get/diva2:757602/FULLTEXT01.pdf

[5] Vianova corporate site, 2015. *Creating Business Value Beyond CSR Reporting.*
http://thevianovagroup.com/2015/07/21/creating-business-value-beyond-csr-reporting

[6] Wamda, 2016. *Should you do it? The benefits and pitfalls of CSR.*
http://www.wamda.com/2016/03/the-potential-benefits-and-pitfalls-of-corporate-social-responsibility-opinion

[7] Clariden Global Insights, 2010. *A Strategic Approach to CSR.*
http://claridenglobal.com/programs/CGArticle_CSRLeadership.pdf

[8] IBM Institute for Business Value, 2009. *Leading a sustainable enterprise.*
http://public.dhe.ibm.com/common/ssi/ecm/gb/en/gbe03226usen/GBE03226USEN.PDF

[9] P. Kotler, N. Lee, 2005. *Corporate Social Responsibility: Doing the Most Good for Your Company and Your Cause.* New Jersey: Wiley.

[10] CECP, 2015. *Giving in Numbers.*
http://cecp.co/pdfs/giving_in_numbers/GIN2015_FINAL_web.pdf

[11] CECP, 2010. *Measuring the Value of Corporate Philanthropy.*
http://cecp.co/pdfs/resources/MVCP_report_singles.pdf

[12] Companies & Causes Canada, 2014. *Canadian Brands Who Do 'Good' Likely to Perform 'Well'.* http://www.companiesandcausescanada.com/canadian-brands-who-do-good-likely-to-perform-well

[13] Cone Communication, 2013. *Global CSR Study.* http://www.conecomm.com/research-blog/2013-cone-communications-echo-global-csr-study

[14] Companies & Causes Canada, 2016. *The Six Types of Corporate Social Initiatives.*
http://www.companiesandcausescanada.com/initiatives

[15] J. Brusseau, G. Deleuze, 2012. *Business Ethics: Three Theories of Corporate Social Responsibility.* http://2012books.lardbucket.org/pdfs/business-ethics.pdf

[16] ISO, 2014. *Discovering ISO 26000.* http://www.iso.org/iso/discovering_iso_26000.pdf

[17] J. Tidd, J. Bessant, 2013. *Managing Innovation.* 5th ed. West Sussex: Wiley

[18] W. Visser, 2005. *Revisiting Carrol's CSR Pyramid.* http://www.waynevisser.com/wp-content/uploads/2012/04/chapter_wvisser_africa_csr_pyramid.pdf

[19] United Nations, 2007. *Industrial Development for 21st Century: Sustainable Development Perspectives.*
https://books.google.com.tr/books?id=DQGy1e9dv_YC&pg=PA387&lpg=PA387&dq=spotlight+on+csr+Malika+Bhandarkar+and+Tarcisio+Alvarez-

Rivero&source=bl&ots=RoPJ3ZwXo6&sig=zxMhLdMZ5L35ZnU0WGx7l4wZbcl&hl=en&sa=X
&ved=0ahUKEwjWuvi78bPNAhUqBcAKHeukB-
wQ6AEIKTAC#v=onepage&q=spotlight%20on%20csr%20Malika%20Bhandarkar%20and%2
0Tarcisio%20Alvarez-Rivero&f=false

[20] HP Speeches, 2003. *Business for Social Responsibility Annual Conference.*
http://www.hp.com/hpinfo/execteam/speeches/fiorina/bsr2003.html

[21] S. Mourougan, 2015. *Corporate Social Responsibility for sustainable business.*
http://iosrjournals.org/iosr-jbm/papers/Vol17-issue5/Version-1/L0175194106.pdf

[22] KPMG, 2014. *Breaking Through: How Corporate Social Innovation Creates Business
Opportunity.*
https://www.kpmg.com/Ca/en/IssuesAndInsights/ArticlesPublications/Documents/5441-
KPMG-Social-Innovation-Report-FY14-web-Final.pdf

[23] L.Y. Chan, 2014. *Corporate Social Responsibility of Multinational Corporations.*
http://digitalcommons.tacoma.uw.edu/cgi/viewcontent.cgi?article=1018&context=gh_theses

[24] Reputation Institute, 2016. *CSR RepTrak 100.*
https://www.reputationinstitute.com/CMSPages/GetAzureFile.aspx?path=~\media\media\docu
ments\global-csr-reptrak-
2016_1.pdf&hash=e6c78476f306bd420872577f9f6ab60e2c52ab8157d283afb665207d95b48
5f8&ext=.pdf

[25] Corporate Responsibility Magazine, 2016. *The 100 Best Corporate Citizens.*
http://www.thecro.com/100-best/the-100-best-corporate-citizens-2

[26] Fair Labor Association corporate site, 2016. *About Us.* http://www.fairlabor.org

[27] Nielsen Global Survey, 2014. *Doing Well by Doing Good.*
http://www.nielsen.com/content/dam/nielsenglobal/apac/docs/reports/2014/Nielsen-Global-
Corporate-Social-Responsibility-Report-June-2014.pdf

[28] BBC News, 2016. *Chobani yoghurt boss gives 10% of his shares to workers.*
http://www.bbc.com/news/business-36146335

[29] The Guardian, 2012. *Unilever's Paul Polman: challenging the corporate status quo.*
http://www.theguardian.com/sustainable-business/paul-polman-unilever-sustainable-living-
plan

[30] M. Porter, M. Kramer, 2006. *Strategy & Society – The Link Between Competitive
Advantage and CSR.*
http://www.issuelab.org/resource/strategy_society_the_link_between_competitive_advantage
_and_corporate_social_responsibility

[31] M. Kramer, 2006. *Strategy & Society.* http://www.ksg.harvard.edu/m-
rcbg/CSRI/events/2006.10.10_Mark%20Kramer_Presentation.pdf

[32] Rangan V. K, Chase L., Karim S., 2015. The Truth about CSR. *Harvard Business
Review.* https://hbr.org/2015/01/the-truth-about-csr

[33] S&P Dow Jones website, 2016. *Dow Jones Sustainability World Index.*
http://eu.spindices.com/indices/equity/dow-jones-sustainability-world-index

[34] Corporate Knights website, 2016. *About Us.* http://www.corporateknights.com/us/about-
us

[35] D'Amato. A., Henderson S., Florence S., 2009. CSR and Sustainable Business – A
Guide to Leadership Tasks and Functions. *Center for Creative Leadership.*
http://insights.ccl.org/wp-content/uploads/2015/04/CorporateSocialResponsibility.pdf

[36] Margolis. J.D., Elfenbeit H.A., Walsh J.P., 2007. *Does It Pay to Be Good . . . and Does It
Matter? A Meta-Analysis of the Relationship between Corporate Social and Financial
Performance.*
https://www.researchgate.net/publication/228273506_Does_It_Pay_to_Be_Good_and_Does_
It_Matter_A_Meta-
Analysis_of_the_Relationship_between_Corporate_Social_and_Financial_Performance

References

[37] The Forum of Sustainable and Responsible Investment, 2014. *US Sustainable, Responsible and Impact Investing Trends.*
http://www.ussif.org/Files/Publications/SIF_Trends_14.F.ES.pdf
[38] Tuan M.T., 2008. *Measuring and/or Estimating Social Value Creation.*
https://docs.gatesfoundation.org/Documents/wwl-report-measuring-estimating-social-value-creation.pdf
[39] Bhatt B., Hebb T., 2013. *Measuring Social Value.* http://carleton.ca/3ci/wp-content/uploads/Social-Metrics-Primer-Sept-20-final-2.pdf
[40] Global Impact Investing Network website, 2016. *IRIS FAQ.*
https://iris.thegiin.org/about/faq#how-are-metrics-developed-and-updated
[41] Social Value UK website, 2016. *What is Social Value?* http://socialvalueuk.org/what-is-sroi
[42] Crowther D., Guler A., 2008. *Corporate Social Responsibility.* Ventus Publishing.
[43] Unilever corporate website, 2015. *Unilever Sustainable Living Plan: Summary of Progress 2015.* https://www.unilever.com/sustainable-living/our-approach-to-a-brighter-future/
[44] Carrots & Sticks, 2016. *Global trends in sustainability reporting regulation and policy.*
https://home.kpmg.com/content/dam/kpmg/pdf/2016/05/carrots-and-sticks-may-2016.pdf
[45] Young W., Hwang K., McDonald S., Oates C.J., 2010. *Sustainable Consumption: Green Consumer Behaviour when Purchasing Products.*
http://onlinelibrary.wiley.com/doi/10.1002/sd.394/abstract
[46] Kramer M., Pfitzer M., Lee P., 2010. *Competitive Social Responsibility: Uncovering the Economic Rationale for Corporate Social Responsibility among Danish Small and Medium Sized Enterprises.* http://www.eogs.dk/graphics/csr/harvard.pdf
[47] Principles for Responsible Investment, 2016. *About the PRI.* https://www.unpri.org/about
[48] Kelly Services, 2009. *Social Responsibility Key to Attracting Top Talent.*
http://ir.kellyservices.com/releasedetail.cfm?releaseid=419383
[49] Body Shop, 2014. *Values Report.*
http://www.thebodyshop.com.au/cms/Assets/About%20Us/VALUES_REPORT_2014_INVALLC020.pdf
[50] Accenture, 2016. *The UN Global Compact-Accenture Strategy CEO Study.*
https://www.accenture.com/us-en/insight-un-global-compact-ceo-study
[51] Oikonomou I., 2011. *Empirical Investigations of the Relationship between Corporate Social and Financial Performance.* http://www.fir-pri-awards.org/files/awardees/2012/PhD_Oikonomou.pdf
[52] Nestle, 2006. *Nestle India Limited.*
https://www.nestle.in/investors/documents/financialmeet_nov29_2006.pdf
[53] Nestle corporate site, 2016. *Nestlé in society: Creating Shared Value and meeting our commitments.* http://www.nestle.com/csv/rural-development-responsible-sourcing/responsible-sourcing/dairy
[54] Hilton corporate site, 2012. *Hilton Worldwide Joins Feeding America and The Global FoodBanking Network to Minimize Food Waste and Alleviate Hunger.*
http://news.hiltonworldwide.com/index.cfm/news/hilton-worldwide-joins-feeding-america-and-the-global-foodbanking-network-to-minimize-food-waste-and-alleviate-hunger
[55] PRNews Online, 2016. *Zuckerberg and Chan Raise the Bar for CSR.*
http://www.prnewsonline.com/water-cooler/2015/12/03/zuckerberg-and-chan-raise-the-bar-for-csr
[56] Whole Foods corporate site, 2012. *5% Day benefiting Road to home Canine Refuge.*http://www.wholefoodsmarket.com/store/event/5-day-benefiting-road-home-canine-refuge
[57] IBM corporate site, 2016. *Corporate Service Corps.*

http://www.ibm.com/ibm/responsibility/corporateservicecorps

[58] BMW corporate site, 2016. *Sustainable Value Report.*
https://www.bmwgroup.com/content/dam/bmw-group-
websites/bmwgroup_com/responsibility/downloads/en/2015/BMW_SVR_2015_RZ_EN_Office
Print.pdf

[59] Anekar K.R., 2012. *CSR Drive of TATA Group.* http://www.iosrjournals.org/iosr-
jbm/papers/ies-mcrc-volume-2/20.pdf

[60] Microsoft blogs, 2016. *How we're putting the Microsoft Cloud to work for the public good.*
http://blogs.microsoft.com/blog/2016/01/19/how-were-putting-the-microsoft-cloud-to-work-for-
the-public-good/#sm.0000iy278mzwgehwsxi15dwhry1ve

[61] S. C. Gherghina, G. Vintilă, D. Dobrescu, 2015. *An Empirical Research on the
Relationship Between Corporate Social Responsibility Ratings and U.S. Listed Companies'
Value.* http://www.ibimapublishing.com/journals/JESR/2015/260450/260450.pdf

[62] S. Johansson, A. Karlsson, C. Hagberg, 2015. *The relationship between CSR and
financial performance.* http://www.diva-portal.org/smash/get/diva2:839031/FULLTEXT01.pdf

[63] Governance & Accountability Institute, 2015. *Flash Report: Eighty One Percent (81%) of
the S&P 500 Index Companies Published Corporate Sustainability Reports in 2015.*
http://www.ga-institute.com/nc/issue-master-system/news-details/article/flash-report-eighty-
one-percent-81-of-the-sp-500-index-companies-published-corporate-sustainabi.html

[64] Business Insider, 2012. *Your iPhone Was Built, In Part, By 13 Year-Olds Working 16
Hours A Day For 70 Cents An Hour.* http://www.businessinsider.com/apple-child-labor-2012-1

[65] TED Talks, 2015. *How to make a profit while making a difference.*
https://www.ted.com/talks/audrey_choi_how_to_make_a_profit_while_making_a_difference/tr
anscript?language=en#t-474679

[66] JUST Capital, 2016. *Perception of Corporate Behaviour.* http://justcapital.com/american-
perceptions

[67] G. Agarwal, 2013. *The Impact of Corporate Social Responsibility on Consumer
Behaviour.* https://air.unimi.it/retrieve/handle/2434/229331/299729/phd_unimi_R08494.pdf

[68] Carnegie council, 2011. *Value vs. Values: The Myth of the Ethical Consumer.*
http://www.policyinnovations.org/ideas/briefings/data/000199

[69] J. Brinkmann, K. Peattie, 2008. *Consumers Ethic Research: Reframing the Debate About
the Consumption for Good.* http://home.bi.no/fgl92025/JB's%20shared%20papers.pdf

[70] T. Green, J. Peloza, 2011. *How does corporate social responsibility create value for
consumers?* http://0-
search.proquest.com.pugwash.lib.warwick.ac.uk/docview/846767837/fulltext/8F9A9AC64710
4B13PQ/1?accountid=14888

[71] L. Moore, D. Webb, K. E. Harris, 2001. *Do consumers expect companies to be socially
responsible? The impact of corporate social responsibility on buying behaviour?* http://0-
search.proquest.com.pugwash.lib.warwick.ac.uk/docview/195909022?accountid=14888

[72] F. L. Simon, 1995. *Global corporate philanthropy: a strategic framework.* http://0-
search.proquest.com.pugwash.lib.warwick.ac.uk/docview/224332755?accountid=14888

[73] A. Selbes, S. Mohamed, 2010. *Consumer Behaviour Analysis in Relation to CSR
Activities of Cosmetics Brands.* http://pure.au.dk/portal-asb-student/files/13393/THESIS

[74] S. Sen, C. B. Bhattacharya, 2001. *Does Doing Good Always Lead to Doing Better?
Consumer Reactions to Corporate Social Responsibility.*
https://faculty.fuqua.duke.edu/~moorman/Marketing-Strategy-Seminar-
2015/Session%2012/Sen%20and%20Bhattacharya%202001.pdf

[75] TED Talks, 2013. *Chris McKnett: The investment logic for sustainability.*
https://www.ted.com/talks/chris_mcknett_the_investment_logic_for_sustainability/transcript?la
nguage=en#t-235160

[76] International Business-Society management book website, 2015. *Leadership and CSR.*

References

http://www.ib-sm.org/LEADERSHIP%20AND%20CSR.pdf

[77] W. Visser, 2011. *The Nature of CSR Leadership - Definitions, Characteristics and Paradoxes.* http://www.ib-sm.org/LEADERSHIP%20AND%20CSR.pdf

[78] McKinsey Insights, 2009. *Making the most of corporate social responsibility.* http://www.mckinsey.com/global-themes/leadership/making-the-most-of-corporate-social-responsibility

[79] McKinsey Insights, 2009. *Valuing corporate social responsibility: McKinsey Global Survey Results.* http://www.mckinsey.com/business-functions/strategy-and-corporate-finance/our-insights/valuing-corporate-social-responsibility-mckinsey-global-survey-results

[80] TCC Group, 2016. *A Framework for Successful Corporate Citizenship.* http://www.tccgrp.com/pubs/tcc_framework_spreads.php

[81] N. K. Kakabadse, A. P. Kakabadse. L. Lee-Davies, 2007. *CSR Leaders road-map.* http://0-search.proquest.com.pugwash.lib.warwick.ac.uk/docview/207991289/fulltextPDF/12E23D3D4FE345DFPQ/1?accountid=14888

[82] Forbes, 2013. *Business Transformation Through Corporate Citizenship.* http://www.forbes.com/sites/brucerogers/2013/08/01/business-transformation-through-corporate-citizenship-how-stanley-litow-keeps-ibm-on-cutting-edge-of-innovation/#1bf5ab1f7462

[83] S. Wu, H. Lin, 2014. *The Correlation of CSR and Consumer Behavior.* http://citeseerx.ist.psu.edu/viewdoc/download?doi=10.1.1.662.9429&rep=rep1&type=pdf

[84] Starbuck corporate site, 2016. *Global Responsibility Report 2015.* http://globalassets.starbucks.com/assets/9248e2c72ff945d9bfb608ced6b7d69d.pdf

[85] Z. Cheers, 2011. *The Corporate Social Responsibility Debate.* http://digitalcommons.liberty.edu/cgi/viewcontent.cgi?article=1229&context=honors

[86] Benefitcorp website, 2016. *What is a Benefit Corporation?* http://benefitcorp.net

[87] The B Team corporate site, 2016. *About B Team.* http://bteam.org/about

[88] US Chamber of Commerce Foundation, 2015. *Impact of CSR Activities on Business Sentiments of Leading Organizations.* Washington: USCC

[89] European CEO, 2016. *Unilever CEO Paul Polman is redefining sustainable business.* http://www.europeanceo.com/business-and-management/unilever-ceo-paul-polman-is-redefining-sustainable-business

[90] W.W. Norton & Company, 2011. *Globalization in a Changing World.* https://www.ibm.com/annualreport/2015/assets/img/2016/02/IBM-Annual-Report-2015.pdf

[91] CSR News, 2015. *GREEN GIANTS: How Smart Companies Turn Sustainability into Billion-Dollar Businesses.* http://www.csrwire.com/press_releases/38273-Book-Release-GREEN-GIANTS-How-Smart-Companies-Turn-Sustainability-into-Billion-Dollar-Businesses

[92] Nike corporate site, 2015. *Sustainable Business Report 2014/2015.* http://s3.amazonaws.com/nikeinc/assets/56356/NIKE_FY14-15_Sustainable_Business_Report.pdf

[93] Sustainable Life Media, 2013. *Nike, Inc. Unveils ColorDry Technology and Facility That Eliminate Water, Chemicals In Dyeing.* http://www.sustainablebrands.com/news_and_views/clean_tech/jennifer-elks/nike-inc-unveils-colordry-technology-facility-eliminate-wate

[94] W. Visser, 2013. *The Age of Responsibility: CSR 2.0 and the New DNA of Business* http://0-eds.a.ebscohost.com.pugwash.lib.warwick.ac.uk/eds/pdfviewer/pdfviewer?sid=07caf646-cc8c-424f-9ae7-9c2ef204d39e%40sessionmgr4007&vid=1&hid=4203

[95] IBM corporate site, 2016. *About On Demand Community.* https://www-01.ibm.com/ibm/ondemandcommunity/home/aboutODC.jsp

[96] World Economic Forum, 2016. *The Global Risks Report.*http://www3.weforum.org/docs/Media/TheGlobalRisksReport2016.pdf

[97] World Economic Forum, 2015. *Engaging Tomorrow's Consumer Project Report.* http://www3.weforum.org/docs/WEFUSA_EngagingTomorrow'sConsumer_ProjectReport2015.pdf

[98] United Nations, 2015. *General Assembly.*http://www.un.org/ga/search/view_doc.asp?symbol=A/RES/70/1&Lang=E

[99] Financial Times, 2006. *A sustainability sweet spot.* http://www.ft.com/cms/s/1/386a1322-0b7c-11db-b97f-0000779e2340.html#axzz4H8xow5iy

[100] J. TIDD, J. BESSANT, 2013. Managing Innovation. 5th ed. West Sussex, Wiley

[101] Journal of Business Ethics, 2015. *Exploring Employee Engagement with (Corporate) Social Responsibility: A Social Exchange Perspective on Organisational Participation.* http://0-eds.a.ebscohost.com.pugwash.lib.warwick.ac.uk/eds/pdfviewer/pdfviewer?sid=e4275c0b-5645-417a-a85b-d77c3b02a2ed%40sessionmgr4009&vid=1&hid=4202

[102] Hemingway C., 2005. *Personal Values as A Catalyst for Corporate Social Entrepreneurship.* http://philpapers.org/archive/HEMPVA-3.pdf

[103] Strandberg Consulting, 2009. *The Role of HRM in CSR.* http://corostrandberg.com/wp-content/uploads/2009/12/csr-hr-management.pdf

[104] University of Leicester, 2016. *Leadership Theories.* http://www.le.ac.uk/oerresources/psychology/organising/page_06.htm

[105] S. J. Zaccaro, C. Kemp, P. Bader, 2003. *Leader Traits and Attributes.* https://us.corwin.com/sites/default/files/upm-binaries/5014_Antonakis_Chapter_5.pdf

[106] B. Bass, 2005. *From Transactional to Transformational Leadership: Learning to Share the Vision.* http://discoverthought.com/Leadership/References_files/Bass%20leadership%201990.pdf

[107] D. Mazutis, C.Zintel, 2015. *Leadership and corporate responsibility: A review of the empirical evidence.* http://www.emeraldinsight.com/doi/full/10.1108/ASR-12-2014-0001

[108] D. A. Waldman, D. S. Siegel , M. Javidan, 2006. *Components of CEO Transformational Leadership and Corporate Social Responsibility.* https://www.researchgate.net/profile/Mansour_Javidan/publication/4771205_Components_of_CEO_Transformational_Leadership_and_Corporate_Social_Responsibility/links/0deec52c1ba7a72699000000.pdf

[109] Ruth V. Aguilera, Deborah E. Rupp, Cynthia A. Williams, Jyoti Ganapathi, 2004. *Putting the S Back In Corporate Social Responsibility: A Multi-Level Theory of Social Change in Organizations.* https://business.illinois.edu/aguilera/pdf/AguileraRuppWilliamsGanapathiAMR2007.pdf

[110] M. H. Tariq, 2015. *Effect of CSR on Employee Engagement.* http://www.indjst.org/index.php/indjst/article/viewFile/64700/50601

[111] P. Mirvis, B. K. Googins, 2006. *Stages of Corporate Citizenship: A Developmental Framework.* http://www.karmayog.org/relateddocumentsoncsr/upload/30192/stages%20of%20corp%20citizenship.pdf

[112] T. Maak, N. M. Pless, 2006. *Responsible leadership in a stakeholder society.* http://eds.a.ebscohost.com.pugwash.lib.warwick.ac.uk/eds/pdfviewer/pdfviewer?sid=05e0f3e9-d087-4796-878e-800bb6c2205f%40sessionmgr4010&vid=1&hid=4111

[113] B. M. Bass, P. Steidlmeier, 1999. *Ethics, Character and Authentic Transformational Leadership Behaviour.* http://s3.amazonaws.com/academia.edu.documents/37341460/ethics-character-and-authentic-transformational-leadership-behavior-1999-bass-and-steidlmeier.pdf?AWSAccessKeyId=AKIAJ56TQJRTWSMTNPEA&Expires=1475478651&Signature=5%2FHY33OIbBmU4tmzljvpWQcfPkc%3D&response-content-disposition=inline%3B%20filename%3DETHICS_CHARACTER_AND_AUTHENTIC_TRANS

References

FORM.pdf

[114] S. O. Idowu, W. L. Filho, 2009. *Global Practices of Corporate Social Responsibility.* Berlin: Springer-Verlag

[115] OECD, 2009. *Annual Report on the OECD Guidelines for Multinational Enterprises: Chapter 6.* http://www.oecd.org/corporate/mne/40889288.pdf

[116] R. K. Yin, 2011. *Qualitative Research from Start to Finish.* New York: Guilford Press

[117] Blogspot, 2014. *Corporate Service Corps, a triple benefit.* http://cscbrazil17.blogspot.co.uk/search?updated-min=2014-01-01T00:00:00%2B01:00&updated-max=2015-01-01T00:00:00%2B01:00&max-results=19

[118] J. Leahy, 2004. *Using Excel for Analysing Survey Questionnaires.* https://learningstore.uwex.edu/Assets/pdfs/G3658-14.pdf

[119] Expats Czech, 2012. *Tomáš Baťa: The Man Behind the Brand.*: https://www.expats.cz/prague/article/prague-business/tomas-bata-the-man-behind-the-brand/

[120] IBM corporate website, 2016. *Responsibility at IBM.* http://www.ibm.com/ibm/responsibility/initiatives.html

[121] FTSE Russell corporate website, 2016. *FTSE4Good Index Series*http://www.ftse.com/products/indices/FTSE4Good

[122] M. Saunders, P. Lewis, A. Thornhill, 2009. *Research methods for business students.* 5th ed. Essex: Pearson

[123] IBM corporate site, 2015. *IBM Annual Report.* https://www.ibm.com/annualreport/2015/assets/img/2016/02/IBM-Annual-Report-2015.pdf

www.ingramcontent.com/pod-product-compliance
Lightning Source LLC
Chambersburg PA
CBHW071312220526
45468CB00001B/347